HOPI
KACHINAS

▾ H ▾ O ▾ P ▾ I ▾
KACHINAS

The Complete Guide
to Collecting Kachina Dolls

by Barton Wright

Northland Publishing

A Justin Company

Dedication

To my wife, Margaret

Table of Contents

Acknowledgments

I AM GRATEFUL to many individuals for their assistance in this publication: the Hopis who contributed their knowledge unselfishly, the dealers who offered comments and criticisms, and certainly those who loaned kachinas from their collections for the fine photography of Peter Bloomer. But most especially I would like to thank my wife for her constant encouragement and much-needed editing.

Introduction

HIGH ON THE MESAS in the arid lands of northeastern Arizona live the Hopi, westernmost of the Pueblo people. A small, peaceful and friendly group, they have occupied their barren mesa tops and farmed their arid but fertile valleys for many centuries. Clinging tenaciously to their marginal land, they have withstood drought, famine and the on-slaught of nomadic raiders. The pressure of Spanish domination, pestilence and, more recently, cultural inundation have diminished but not destroyed their traditional pattern of life.

The Hopi are bound together by their religion, a multi-stranded cord uniting them to withstand the hazards of a harsh environment and in rebuffing foreign incursions. Their religion is both their bulwark and the lure that attracts forces that would destroy them.

Prior to the arrival of the Spanish, over 400 years ago, the Hopi villages were one of the urban centers in the Southwest. To the non-Pueblo Indians this meant not only a trading center and a storehouse of food to be raided if one were short, but a place of power where men could control the vagaries of the real and supernatural worlds. This mystique persists today as other Indians attribute greater healing power to Hopi doctors or a knowledge of things beyond average comprehension.

To the intruding Spanish, however, Hopi religion was a challenge to be overcome and a belief to be destroyed as quickly as possible so that Catholicism could be substituted. Circumstances such as distance and the logistics of supply for Spanish punitive expeditions, as well as political guile on the part of the Hopi, allowed them to maintain their religious freedom. Their less fortunate Pueblo neighbors to the east, closer to the new Spanish center, were overrun and their religion diluted or driven underground.

With the arrival of the Americans came a new threat. While Hopi religion became less and less a challenge to proselytizing Christians it became more of a curiosity to attract and edify visitors. Countless tourists in carnival mood made the trek to the remote villages to watch the most famous of all Hopi ceremonies, the Snake Dance, as well as other dances. Despite the adversities the Hopi continued to practice their time-honored religion with unabated zeal.

The driving force of Hopi religion is the urgent need for water in any form, as rain for farming, for drinking water in the springs, or snow to replenish the land. Water is forever the primary motivation. To survive in this waterless land the Hopi developed a complex religion to secure supernatural assistance in fulfilling their needs. Through the ages rain ritual was elaborated and joined to planting ritual, the growth of corn and Hopi melded, the successful rites of neighbors were added to further compound the ceremonies until the present complexity of Hopi belief was achieved.

One element of this multi-faceted religion is the Kachina Cult, with every Hopi past the age of ten being an initiated member. The basic concept of the cult is that all things in the world have two forms, the visible object and a spirit counterpart, a dualism that balances mass and energy. Kachinas are the spirit essence of everything in the real world. Their existence is inferred from the steam which rises from food and whose loss does not change the form of the food, to the mist rising from a spring on a cold morning or the cloud which forms above a mountain top. As the breath of a dying Hopi departs it also must join the other mist-beings in a spirit world, the exact counterpart of the real Hopi world but with different powers. Thus when the clouds form over the mountain tops and drift over the Hopi villages it is the rain-bringing kachinas who are there. The clouds hide not only the faces of the Hopi's departed ancestors who, taking pity on their grandchildren, are bringing them rain, but an almost infinite variety of kachinas who have other functions beside rain bringing.

This multitude of spirits range from Star Kachinas to Ash Kachi-

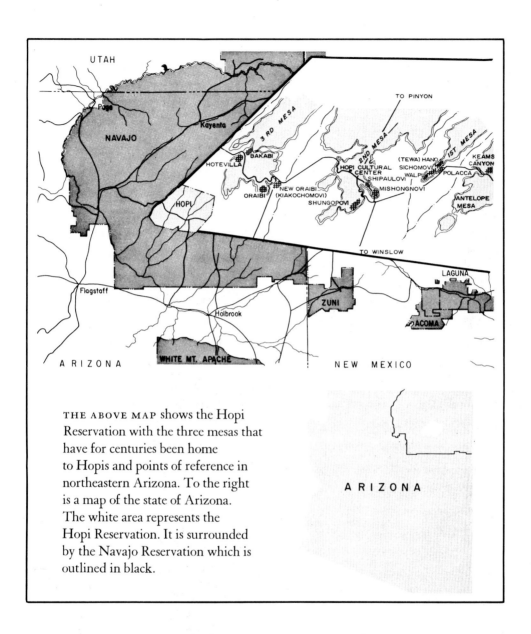

THE ABOVE MAP shows the Hopi
Reservation with the three mesas that
have for centuries been home
to Hopis and points of reference in
northeastern Arizona. To the right
is a map of the state of Arizona.
The white area represents the
Hopi Reservation. It is surrounded
by the Navajo Reservation which is
outlined in black.

3

nas. They represent game, domestic plants and animals, wild foods, birds, insects, even death itself is given kachina form. The creative force of the sun and the abstract power inherent in neighboring tribes are visualized as kachinas. Many others were not conceived by the Hopi but arose among their Pueblo neighbors and were adopted because of their efficacy. These kachinas visit the clusters of Hopi villages on their separate mesas from the end of December till the end of July when they disappear for several months. The Hopi do not worship these kachinas but rather treat them as friends or partners who are interested in Hopi welfare. Because it is not easy to interact with the kachinas in their insubstantial form it remains a simple matter to give them shape and personality by impersonating them. Through paint, symbols, actions and costume they give substance to the immaterial, becoming in the process intermediaries between the two halves of the Hopi world. Hence the Hopi men who don kachina masks in dance and ritual are believed to be invested by a specific kachina spirit. In this condition of being part human and part kachina the needs of the people for rain, corn or game can be more clearly communicated.

The kachina season begins in late December with a ritual opening of the kivas. These kivas are underground ceremonial chambers which are believed to be entryways to the Spirit or Underworld. There are usually several in each village incorporating most of the men as kiva members. Once the way is opened kachinas will come and go from the kivas until the path is again closed to them toward the end of July. The Hopi waste scant time categorizing their supernaturals, finding it far more fruitful to enjoy their kachinas and the benefits they bring. This propensity may be the despair of ethnologists but it does little to hamper the practice of Hopi religion. Within the span of time that they are present the kachinas still help renew the world and ready it for the coming season of growth. They will initiate the Hopi children, insure growth and abundance and, as always, bring moisture. They will bring discipline to some and give direction to all in proper behavior, but their greatest gift will be happiness, good health and a long life.

There are three main ceremonies given by the Hopi at the present time. In late December the Soyal or the opening of the kachina season begins when one or two kachinas emerge from the kivas much in the manner of sleepy early risers in a household fumbling about their necessary chores. As these important chief kachinas move about they perform rites to strengthen individual, clan and village in the coming year before returning to their kivas. As the year progresses the kivas burgeon with kachinas dancing in the below-ground warmth. With the arrival of the false spring of February comes the second great ceremony, the Powamu, when the world is readied for the new season of growth. Out of the kivas pour throngs of kachinas great and small, protected in their activities by guards and warriors and followed as they walk through the villages by a froth of clowns. During this period the children are initiated into the Kachina Cult and readied for their growing season just as the land will be.

Following the Powamu the cold returns and for a short period dances are again held in the kivas, slowly merging into the plaza dances as true spring appears and the weather moderates. These dances are for the growth of corn, the mainspring of Hopi existence, and for the increase of both wild and domestic plants and animals. Lines of kachinas enter the plazas dancing on all four sides and then retiring to rest while clowns cavort to both entertain and educate the audience. If the dancers are all of the same kind of kachina it will be called a Line Dance but if they are a variety it becomes a Mixed Dance. Either of these may be accompanied by kachinas who dance with exaggerated steps and stay apart from the lines, the Side Dancers.

Dances start in the morning and continue until dusk with pauses only for rest and eating. Although each dance follows a traditional pattern, songs are composed afresh for each year's performance and the popularity of a kachina may rest on the people's enjoyment of the songs much in the manner that a waltz might achieve popularity in one form but not another. The dance begins, not at a specific time, but when they are ready and continues through the day. It is usually presented eight to twelve times during a day and may be given two days in succession.

The kachina season draws to a close as the growing season places increasing demands on the men's time. The final ceremony comes in mid-summer at about the time that early corn matures and is a thanksgiving rite for another season of growth. The kachinas dance once more bringing presents of entire stalks of corn or reeds with attached gifts for the youngsters. The dance ends with throngs of Hopi men and women walking down the line of dancers and casting corn flour or meal as a prayer to the kachinas. The kachinas are thanked for their assistance and urged not to forget their friends the Hopi. Then with one final ritual they are sent home to their mountain peaks, disappearing into the kivas until a new year returns.

Although the Hopi are a matriarchy, the women do not have the same degree of contact with the supernatural that the men possess. Consequently a subsidiary system has arisen that fulfills this need. The men who impersonate kachinas and dance in the plazas, carve small wooden replicas of their kachina appearance and present these to infants and all ages of females. These images are given when the men, usually relatives, are impersonating the kachinas. This carved and painted figure is called a *tihu* by the Hopi and a kachina "doll" by others. It is not a doll, a plaything for children, but an effigy or small part of the kachina it represents. It bears a portion of the kachina spirit's power just as a child bears resemblance to its parents. Nevertheless the term "kachina doll" has become the name of this object rather than *tihu*. Boys receive kachina dolls only when they are infants in arms and not truly separate from their mothers. Girls who are approaching marriageable age receive the majority although a mother or an occasional grandmother may receive one from her husband. These dolls are often spoken of, in the literature, as mnemonic devices but this seems far less likely than that they represent an effort to bring the benefits of association with the kachina supernaturals to the women. Once the doll is presented it is not treated as a toy but rather as a valued possession and is hung from a beam or wall in the house out of harm's way.

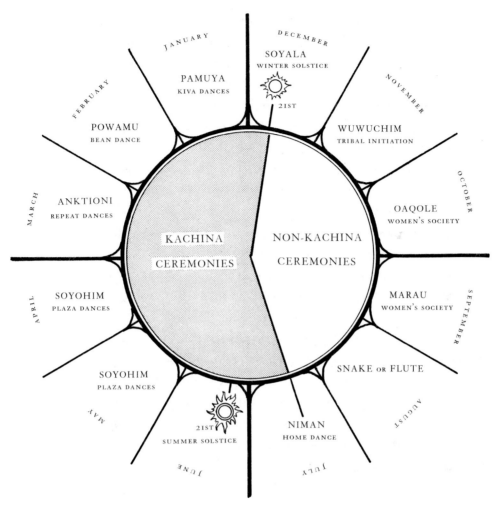

Calendar of major Hopi ceremonies

The first ethnographers on seeing these dolls were intrigued and attempted to buy them. The Hopi resisted this as best they were able in the face of the dominant group. Nevertheless, pressures were brought to bear that at first forced them to sell and then induced them to continue because of economic gain once the initial resistance was overcome. Although many dolls are now carved on a semi-commercial basis there are few carvers who do not have reservations about which dolls they will carve and how they should be treated. These dolls, made for sale, may be given as presents during a dance as readily as ones made for that purpose.

Kachinas and kachina dolls are not recent innovations anywhere within the pueblo world although their history is obscure. The Spanish wrote in the 1500s of seeing hideous images of the devil, undoubtedly kachina dolls, hung in pueblo homes, and of the idolatrous dances these misguided pagans held, surely kachina dances. That the kachina cult existed prior to the Spanish invasion is supported by archaeological evidence of pottery designs from the late 1300–1400s with identifiable kachina likenesses. Murals of painted supernaturals on kiva walls and painted slabs with images resembling kachinas have been excavated from even earlier ruins. The earliest finds to date are of perishable material from caves in southern New Mexico and Arizona indicating the presence of the kachina concept. How this belief with its accompanying paraphernalia developed and spread to many different tribes during the thousand years of its known existence is buried in the countless unexcavated ruins throughout the Southwest. Ethnologists and historians found that all Pueblo people regardless of racial group possessed kachina dolls.

Keresan or Shoshonean, Zuñi or Tewa, Tiwa or Towa, all made dolls, only their form and number varied. Most of the pueblos such as Acoma and its neighbors to the east produce kachina dolls with cylindrical bodies and stylized heads. The image is usually draped with a bit of cloth and strings with beads of turquoise or shell wrapped about the body. A few feathers complete the doll. Despite this simplicity of appearance the dolls carry the same religious connotations of the more elaborately dressed and carved western dolls and are infinitely more difficult to find.

The Zuñi and Hopi are the two groups best known for their dolls. Zuñi produces far fewer dolls than the Hopi and of less variety. Their carved kachinas are distinguishable in usually having movable limbs and tiny feet and in being dressed in miniature clothing. The dolls are almost always taller and thinner than those carved by the Hopi. Along the western fringe of the Pueblo people, kachina dolls received their greatest attention, proliferating into hundreds of types through the imagination of the Hopi. These dolls, until recently, were rigidly carved and wore painted garb and were squat, blocky figures compared to the Zuñi dolls. It is these throngs of brightly colored, easily secured kachina dolls of the Hopi which have instigated the majority of collections.

A kachina doll begins with a search for the proper wood from which the image is to be made, for not just any wood will suffice. The wood must be the root of the water-seeking cottonwood tree, and it must be thoroughly dried and seasoned. Formerly Hopi men journeyed west to the Little Colorado and searched the banks and falls for roots of trees swept down by the river. A favored location was Grand Falls, where windrows of these scoured roots were racked up by previous floods to dry for decades. Selection was merely a matter of picking the best piece of wood and carrying it home. However, recent years have brought many changes to this procedure. Today there are more kachina carvers searching for wood, and they are carving to supply a far greater need brought about by an increased Hopi population as well as the expanded market of collectors. The supply of cottonwood root that was adequate for the Hopi could not sustain the additional demands of the commercial market, and the local supply was soon exhausted. An occasional tree is still swept down the river for a Hopi to find, but in general the roots now come from all over the Southwest. Here again the supply is short for many others, Mexican-American santeros, Anglo carvers and other Pueblo people also use the wood to carve.

Efforts to supply substitute woods have met with dismal failure. Aspen wood, which is locally available and has many similar characteristics, was rejected out of hand. Easily carved balsa wood has been tried but is considered so inferior that only the most desperate Hopi will use it. Occasionally a carver will be reduced to using a cottonwood limb but the wood is heavy and hard to work and is consequently seldom used.

As the local supplies of wood became inadequate the Hopi carvers have extended their areas of collection throughout the Southwest, paying for any wood that they could not salvage on their own. Prices for a running foot of prime cottonwood root ranging from six to eight inches in diameter cost $1.50 in 1965. The same piece of wood in 1977 will bring nearly $50.00.

Once the wood is collected the roots that are damp or still partially green are set aside for further drying over a stove or some other warm, dry location. Pieces with the greatest diameter are hoarded for larger dolls, smaller ones are used for arms, legs and gear as virtually none of the carvers make the entire doll from a single piece of wood other than the flat infant dolls or *puchtihu*.

When the carver is ready to begin he selects a suitable length of wood and cuts it with a hand saw to the proper length. Formerly this was done with a knife or a flake of stone but steel tools have replaced all of the native implements used in carving. The basic torso is also outlined with the hand saw. Cuts are made at the neck, below the arms, at the base of the kilt and often upward between the legs. The carver then switches to either a hatchet or the most favored tools, a butcher knife and mallet, to roughly shape the contours of the head, the ruff about the neck, and the body and legs. For the difficult closed-in areas such as under the kilt or around the mask, carvers use chisels of various sizes and a selection of wood rasps. The carver completes the intricate carving of details such as the single threads of a sash or the delicate structure of spruce boughs or fingernails with an assortment of worn-down pocket knives or similar tools. At the same time the arms, various bits of costume and gear, and occasionally in the more active dolls, the legs, are carved separately. These are then attached with pegs and white glue and any cracks filled in with wood paste. The entire doll is then sanded to a smooth finish with the modern sandpapers that have replaced the bits of sandstone formerly used for smoothing.

In 1857, the first doll was collected from the Hopi by Dr. Palmer, a United States Army surgeon, who presented it to the National Museum. Other early examples are to be found in the American Museum of Natural History and the Heye Foundation in New York, the Field Museum in Chicago and the *Museum für Volkerkunde* in Berlin. These charming early dolls reflect the simpler technology of that period and the effort required to produce such a carving. The arms were formed as an integral part of the torso and the legs often barely separated with merely an indication of the fact. Occasionally in the larger dolls the arms and other appurtenances would be separately carved and then attached with tiny wooden pins, for glue was not a common commodity among the Hopi of that period.

In later years an effort to mass-produce kachina dolls brought a superficial resemblance to these traditional dolls with the so-called "lathe-turned" doll. This type of doll was made with a series of saw cuts from a rounded piece of wood and the arms were consequently bent around the body and remained unseparated. The lathe-turned doll, however, has none of the charm of the traditional carvings, being instead a completely mechanical exercise. Fortunately this type of doll was a shortlived venture.

Upon completion of the carving and sanding of the kachina doll the next step is to paint the doll with a coating of clay. Cottonwood root must be primed, for the wood is quite porous. This clay is found in various locations in the valleys between the Hopi mesas. The men bring home large chunks which are then broken up into a container of water and allowed to soak. As the clay softens the coarse grit sinks to the bottom, leaving the finer clay particles in suspension. The water evaporates, reducing the fluid to a thick, creamy clay that is then painted on the doll, sealing the pores in the wood and giving the doll an even gray-white surface or ground upon which to paint. There is an increasing tendency in recent years to buy commercial gesso or acrylic substitutes to coat the dolls. Both of these products giver greater brilliance to the paint. However, they also produce a slick plastic quality to the doll that is not necessarily an attribute.

Paint has always been of great importance to the kachina carvers, for it answers several purposes. The Hopi recognize six cardinal directions, each with an associated color. North is indicated by yellow, the west by blue-green, the south red and the east white. To these directional colors are added black for the zenith and all colors or gray for the nadir. Consequently the colors applied to a doll may symbolize the direction from which the kachina comes and by association its function. The body color of the kachina may also indicate whether it is a beneficial or a dangerous and fearsome spirit. These traditional color combinations for body paint and mask symbols formerly were more meaningful than are recognized today. Because of this tradition today's carvers feel constrained to paint all of the details of costume and body. It is not uncommon to find the most minute of dolls with every element as carefully painted as though the doll were of regular size.

Both paint and equipment have developed over the past century just as tools have changed. The early yucca fiber brush which was dragged along the surface of the wood has given way to the finest of sable brushes, but it is probably paint that has changed most radically. All of the earliest paints were of native materials, mineral paints from oxides of iron, copper ores and colored clays as well as vegetable dyes. A wide range of hues was possible although the majority of all dolls utilized less than a dozen of these colors. With the introduction of American goods, available from government agent, trader and teacher came ink, bluing, watercolors and oil-based paints. Each of these seems to have been tried and discarded as its inadequacies were recognized, with the exception of tempera or poster paint. These opaque watercolors not only bonded well with the underlying clay ground but produced a fine, clear color. The only exception was the lack of the beautiful blue-green which could be obtained with copper carbonate. Consequently, this native color persisted well into the twentieth century before it was supplanted by tempera. For nearly fifty years tempera remained the favorite paint, easy to obtain and most like the native paint, its only drawback being a tendency to dry up rather quickly and to slack or oxidize. This slacking of the surface paint caused the colors to rub off on anything with which they came in contact. To overcome this difficulty, carvers in the 1950s began to use the new aerosol spray cans, trying everything from hair spray to charcoal fixative to set the paint. This episode came to an end with the introduction of acrylic paints, which were easily applied and brilliant in hue. They also remained moist longer in the arid climate than had the old tempera paints. In addition they did not oxidize or rub off and are used today by the majority of carvers.

Upon completion of the painting and the subsequent drying, the final parts are added. Rattles, bow and arrows, crooks and other gear are worked from wood and placed in the hand or upon the heads of the dolls. However, it is in the costume that Hopi ingenuity is pushed to its utmost. Where the historic carver was content to symbolize or simplify the carving, the modern carver pushes realism to its utmost. To accomplish this he has but to turn to the treasure chest of contemporary American goods wherein lies an incredible profusion of useful items. From this inexhaustible supply he draws those things which most closely simulate the necessary object. An example of this is the development of the ruff on kachina dolls. A kachina wears a ruff of either cloth, fur, or spruce greens about his neck to hide the base of the mask. The doll's ruff is a duplication in miniature. However, when real spruce was used for the doll the foliage soon turned brown and dropped off, leaving only the tiny branches. This was not a matter of concern to the Hopi until they began to sell the dolls and collectors demanded something more permanent. The Hopi first carved the ruffs of wood in a tubular form and painted them green. Later ruffs were painted with tiny branches and varying shades of green to add to their realistic appearance. This was soon followed by notching to give the appearance of the irregularity of branches. The process was time-consuming and substitutes were sought. Among the first was imitation greenery of glassy-looking plastic which did not truly resemble foliage and cheapened the doll's appearance. A better material was dyed seaweed from the English Channel which first appeared in architectural supplies and later in hobby shops. It resembled the desired spruce boughs and was quite durable. The last step has been the use of green yarn cut into short lengths which are tied about the neck with the ends projecting and resemble evergreens more than any of the earlier efforts.

The shells worn by doll and dancer which formerly came through trade or expeditions to the Pacific Coast or the Gulfs of California and Mexico are now derived from a worldwide market. Minute shells from the Indian Ocean or the South Pacific may be found adorning many a kachina doll in some little-known trading post on the reservation.

Leather and fur have followed the same expansion of supply, and where formerly bits of mouse or squirrel skin became hair on the heads and backs of certain kachinas one may now find seal skin. Fur coats given to the Hopi by well-meaning individuals as often as not find that their gift has been converted to cape or collar for a variety of kachina dolls. On some of the more expensive dolls tiny white ermine tails have been used for fur collars or tail pieces. Buckskin has been replaced by suede. Miniature leather gatos and concho belts are decorated with bits of real silver and turquoise or embossed carpet tacks. The variety is almost endless. Cloth also is being utilized to the maximum and colored felts and flannels, ribbons and silks are converted to clothing, sashes and bandoleers. In some instances the cloth is actually woven or embroidered but in most cases it is simply painted with the proper design.

The final step in the adornment of the doll is the feathers. Formerly religion dictated which feathers were to be used. Kachinas wore the down of eagles on their heads to represent the clouds and their moisture floating overhead much as the eagle soared above. Warrior kachinas were adorned with the feathers of birds of prey. They wore the hard black plumes of the wings of eagles and wisps of owl fluff to aid their night vision. Prairie falcon, red-tailed hawk and crow were all used on the proper dolls. Upon the kachinas who bring flowers, gentle rain and the greenery of summer, are found feathers which represent the color and brightness of that time. The yellow of the Tawa Mana (Sun Girl or Oriole) shines on the foreheads of many kachinas. The scarlet tail feathers of the military macaw and the always-astonishing color of the mountain bluebird or the greens of the chat or warbler are mixed with the down of eagle and turkey to represent the colors of summer. The selection of these feathers is now determined by the Fish and Game Service of the United States Department of the Interior. The reason for this unhappy circumstance stems from a law passed many years ago to protect egrets and other endangered birds. Recently that law was enormously expanded and rigidly enforced, and kachina carvers who transgress it now face stiff fines or prison sentences for the use of these feathers.

Kachina makers are often both religious and commercial carvers as the dolls are suitable for either purpose. In earlier times they used the feathers left from ceremonies for their dolls. Nowadays, however, they must use the feathers of domestic fowl, sparrows or starlings due to the augmented regulation which protects *all* birds, even those with bounties paid for their elimination. In consequence the doll makers attempt to carve wooden feathers or use the ridiculously inadequate substitutes if they continue to carve. The enforcement of this law in recent years has almost eradicated kachina carving as the traders are fearful of the methods employed by government officials in enforcing the law. While this is a loss of heritage for the Hopi and of esthetic enjoyment by artists and all others appreciative of native crafts, it goes even farther. Because possession of feathers is illegal many genuine old kachinas bought years ago are being shorn of their "illicit" feathers thus destroying much of the significance of the dolls.

Collectors have been intrigued with kachina dolls from the first moment of American contact by army men and government agents. These individuals purchased the kachina dolls against strong protest by the Hopi who had no desire to sell the dolls and in fact expressed an active aversion to the suggestion. Nevertheless, the new visitors speaking from a position of authority with an army accompanying them overcame this reluctance and bought some of the dolls. From that moment onward the demand for dolls and the number of collectors increased. These initial collections too often were simply curiosities, memorabilia from past exploits that found their way into museums and archives. They are fragments of a culture with no documentation, no maker's names or description of functions, often they do not even have geographical locations and consequently are almost meaningless. It is a fact these bits of data were seldom given more than passing attention until the middle 1930s. Several good ethnologists who studied the Hopi during the 1890s did record ceremonies and at least secured a name for the doll and a minimum of information, but never the maker or his village, a curious oversight.

The great surge of interest in Indian crafts that swept the United States during the first part of the twentieth century did not emphasize kachina dolls, undoubtedly because the Hopi were still loath to sell their dolls and because of the cultural emphasis among the Hopi that demanded anonymity of craftsmen. There was no conscious effort by any man to compete or be recognized as unique. In fact, the unusual carver or artist prior to World War II was deliberately submerged. This system began to disintegrate as the Hopi took up wage work and moved off the reservation into neighboring towns. There they carved dolls to supplement their wages and almost as a hobby to occupy their evenings. Many of the townspeople who became their customers and collected the dolls urged them to sign their work and receive recognition. Jimmie Kewanwytwea at the Museum of Northern Arizona was undoubtedly one of the best-known carvers and apparently the first to put his initials on his work. He did this only after repeated urgings by Mrs. Harold S. Colton, the wife of the founder of the museum. For this he was thoroughly castigated by the other Hopi who felt that the maker of a doll should be unknown. Otherwise the recipients of the dolls would know that their relatives had carved it and would not believe that they came directly from the kachina spirits. Jimmie "K," realizing that the market for his dolls was not the same as that of the Hopi on the reservation, persisted in signing his dolls until his death in the sixties. He thus became one of the first commercial carvers of kachina dolls.

A few other doll makers from this period became known, such as Porter Timeche at Grand Canyon and Chief Joe Secakuku who owned and operated a small curio store at Holbrook. In addition to carving dolls of his own he sold the dolls of others as well as many kinds of Hopi crafts. Tawaquoptewa, the chief at Old Oraibi, carved kachina dolls so unique that they are instantly recognizable although they were never signed. The old man believed that as *kikmongwi* or spiritual leader of Old Oraibi he should not carve and sell dolls, and yet he needed them as presents for his friends and an occasional bit of money. Consequently he carved dolls that were jumbled, the symbols of one being placed on the body of another, as well as inventing markings, costumes and names. These dolls are now collector's items. Another individual who carved unusual dolls was Otto Pentewa of New Oraibi. Otto chose wood from distorted roots that suggested certain kachinas to him. From these roots came dolls of considerable humor who appeared to bend and dance to some unheard chant. These dolls are also much sought after by knowledgeable collectors.

An occasional carver of this period produced dolls with such distinctive characteristics that they may be instantly recognized and yet no name has ever been attached to the carvings. In part this was due to the secretive nature of kachina carving in this earlier time and in part to a lack of records. The main reason, however, was that they were not considered as ethnographic or artistic items of great worth. As this attitude changes it is reflected in the prices paid for these carvings. At the beginning of this century prices ranged from twenty-five cents to the rare two or three-dollar variety. The depression times of the 1930s and the increasing anxieties of approaching war kept the prices minimal with ten dollars being the upper limit.

When World War II came it took most of the young men away from the reservation leaving only the elders to keep the ceremonies and crops alive and to care for the families. Rationing of gas and supplies made travel virtually impossible and dealers could not reach the craftsmen nor could the craftsmen come to the almost nonexistent market. The returning veterans, in the decade following World War II, brought home new technologies and ideas other than those tribally imposed. The way had already been opened for commercial carving of kachina dolls. This was further encouraged by the crowds attending events such as the Gallup Intertribal Ceremonial and the Flagstaff Pow Wow as well as an increasing awareness of Indian crafts. Guilds and cooperative ventures as well as many individual craftsmen have their beginnings during this decade. At this time the standard price for kachina dolls was one dollar an inch.

The sixties and seventies brought an ever-increasing change in carving as well as prices. The individuals who were carvers were quick to respond to any economic advantage and to note that a little more movement or action in a doll brought increased sales. This precipitated a trend toward ever-greater realism, not alone in costume and mask but in anatomy and motion. The carvers vied with each other in putting more movement into their work and the result was the "action" doll where all of the body motions of the kachina dancers are duplicated in the carving of the kachina doll.

The change to action poses in dolls precipitated yet another change, that of support of the doll. Where formerly the traditional dolls hung in rigid poses from rafters and walls suspended by strings about their necks, the action doll required a base to prevent the breakage of extended arms and legs. Some carvers, like Sankey George, solved the problem by making the feet overly large in an effort to support the doll in a standing position. Other carvers glued scraps of board to the bottom of the feet to make the doll stand erect. Fortunately these superficial solutions were soon replaced with neat cottonwood root sections, often with the name of the doll and its maker written on the bottom side.

The prices, which had been rising slowly in reflection of the changes in carving, took a formidable jump at this time, partially because of the increasing awareness of Indian crafts as art on the part of the American public. By 1974 the values had risen to over one thousand dollars for the more elaborately carved action dolls.

The drive toward realistic carving brought with it experimentation with new products and ushered in the use of acrylic paints and sprays. Among the first "action" doll carvers of this period were Willard Sakiestewa, Henry Shelton and his brother, Peter. Peter, a recognized artist at the time, may have drawn upon this expertise to introduce the use of acrylic paints for dolls.

As the public interest and demand for dolls increased so did the number of carvers bringing in an ever-wider range of talent. Names such as Alvin James Makya, Arthur Holmes, Clifford Bahnimptewa, Earl Yoywytewa and others became known for their unique carvings. Other carvers such as Dick Pentewa, Jeffer Joseph, Arthur Bilagody and Emil Pooley changed their carving styles very little and continued to produce excellent traditional dolls. In addition, a few Hopi women began to carve dolls for the first time in remembered history.

Kachina fads have always been present among the Hopi and are dependent upon the success of the dances and songs given in the plaza. If these were popular the dolls that were carved immediately thereafter would most often be of the same type. However, the new market and the demands of the non-Hopi for kachina dolls brought with it different fads. Some of these were of momentary interest while others have lasted for years, but none were based on kachina performances.

An early minor fad which has reappeared cyclically is the jumping doll. A Hopi clown or other kachina is carved and jointed in the manner of a puppet and then strung on crossed strings like a common European jumping toy. When the strings are pulled apart and relaxed the doll leaps and cavorts about. The first individual to produce this type of doll among the Hopi appears to have been a First Mesa man named Ben Seeni. At least no earlier examples have so far been documented.

However, interest in the doll fades rapidly but it is then re-discovered within a few years and again enjoys a brief flurry of popularity.

In the middle sixties a few extra large dolls were sold for excellent prices and the immediate result was a flood of ever-larger kachinas. Most of these dolls had little to recommend them other than size, for the rendering of details tended to become less well executed rather than the opposite. Some of these dolls were immense, ranging in size from three to five feet, while others done on special orders were even larger. The idea of large kachina dolls was not new as there are photographs of carvings of this size from the late nineteenth century. The fad of gigantism was merely the reflection of an economic stimulus and one that fortunately was short-lived as few collectors had the necessary space. As interest waned in gigantism an opposite interest arose in miniature dolls. Silas Roy and his brother Rousseau, Alfred Fritz and Gene Kewanvuyaoma among others began to produce dolls ranging in height from three to six inches. Mary Shelton, probably the best of the miniature carvers, once produced a Rattle Kachina half an inch in height with a completely decorated sash about its waist. Another woman carver, Barbara Drye, makes elaborately costumed dolls ranging in height from four to six inches. Many of the miniature carvers have added a further innovation by clustering their dolls in sets upon pieces of sandstone or dried wood to produce an effect similar to a diorama. Again the multiple figure set is not new as Snake Dance groups were common in the 1920s. Many of these Snake Dancer sets are very well done and have as many as twenty-five figures that are ten to twelve inches high.

The demands of collectors have produced several other major effects on the doll market. The demand for clowns, whether in response to their humor or the difficulty of remembering and pronouncing other kachina names, has given an undue emphasis to this minor group of dolls. It is becoming increasingly difficult to secure any dolls other than a few limited types. These dolls are common because they sell better. The Koshari, Koyemsi, Ho-e and the infinitely adaptable Chuku are the preferred dolls, and carvers such as Alfred Fritz, Wilbert Talashoma, Carl Sulu, Ira and Wilfred Tewawina produce marvelous carvings that are examples of Hopi visual humor. The Squash Kachina is also a favorite with collectors and carries an appeal almost as great although it is not a clown. Another group that is currently popular are the ogres such as Chaveyo and Soyok Wuhti.

Unfortunately this specialized demand is having serious effects on the carving of dolls. Most carvers do not have a large repertoire of dolls which they carve. They learn a limited number from other Hopi, by memorizing the kachinas they see at dances, or by observing them as dolls. Consequently the effect on future production is both through the number of examples and by object lesson as to what is saleable. This adverse effect is reducing the variety of dolls at an alarming rate.

The pornographic doll is another type, other than clowns, which appears to be on the increase. Pornography as such is not native to the Hopi. Sex and all other natural functions are not taboo subjects but are recognized as a fact of life and receive no special attention. Hopi humor, however, runs to the earthy side and Hopi clowns may perform many acts which would be considered by the non-Hopi as totally obscene. One sacred kachina may appear with a prayer feather tied to his penis while others may parade the plaza with their buttocks painted red or mimic the act of copulation. They are not greeted with embarrassed laughter, averted eyes or smart remarks but with respect. Both Kokopelli and Kokopel' Mana are given undue importance in the Hopi pantheon because of this non-Hopi interest. Hopi carvers will continue to supply these dolls in increasingly explicit detail as long as there is interest among those who are titillated by such dolls.

This type of demand leads to the carving of a wide range of non-kachina figures as well, such as the Mountain Spirit dancers of the Apache, society chiefs of the Hopi, Snake dancers, social dancers such as the Butterfly and Buffalo, and participants in women's societies. Some individuals have asked for aberrant dolls with removable masks. Other carvers have produced images of Hopi men, women, brides, farmers, "princesses" and others which are not painted and in consequence are much closer to true sculpture. Some collectors coming in contact with the enormous variety of kachinas often ask for non-existent dolls which of course will be supplied if they persist in their requests. This appears to be the manner in which the folktale of the field mouse who fought and defeated the prairie falcon became a "kachina doll." The tale was translated by a school teacher on the reservation, Edward A. Kennard, and illustrated by a Hopi, Fred Kabotie, and then published by the United States Government. A purchaser of the book was entranced with the Field Mouse who went to war and asked for a "kachina" doll of him. Today one may find both Field Mouse and Mickey Mouse sold as kachina dolls when in actuality neither have ever been danced as kachinas nor do they exist in the Hopi pantheon. In another instance an atmospheric physicist working in the region decided that he would like a Cloud Kachina. Despite the fact that many forms of Cloud Kachinas existed his request was stated in such a manner that the doll produced bore little resemblance to any kachina figure. Fortunately this doll did not catch on.

A persistent delusion by collectors is that it is possible to have a complete collection of all the kachina dolls made. But dolls are an art form that is constantly changing. It is an art practiced by many artisans who live in twelve different reservation villages as well as neighboring towns. The dolls they produce are carved and painted within their conception of the kachina type. However, some carvers have excellent memories and others do not, even though they are striving in virtually every instance to produce an accurate kachina image. The possibilities of variation within specific modes of innovation are such that any given kachina should be considered a cluster of characteristics rather than a single "true" image. Because of this and the fact that they are carving to satisfy their own criteria and not ours, there is little cause for them to produce a fake or "tourist" doll.

Nevertheless there are fake kachina dolls for sale in the Southwest, virtually all of them made by non-Indians. The majority are easily recognized because of the materials from which they are made such as balsa wood or pine. Those originating in foreign countries are usually very simplified forms with paper designs pasted on the wood. Others are touted as being genuine wood, of Indian style, or other wording which implies authenticity without actually guaranteeing the product. Reputable shops do not carry these items. The majority of these stores are members of the IACA, the Indian Arts and Crafts Association. This organization of traders and craftsmen works to eradicate the fakes and guarantee the purchaser authentic merchandise with a money-back policy.

As is the case with any art form, change occurs, more slowly perhaps than many contemporary art schools, but still a constant variation through time and between villages. As an example, the Mudhead or Koyemsi, one of the simplest of three to four hundred known kachinas, has five major types with over thirty known varieties of these forms. Hence it is far better to collect a particular class of kachina dolls such as clowns, warriors or chief kachinas, for even here there is sufficient variation to challenge the most ardent collector. The current trend of signing dolls offers yet another avenue of collection, the acquisition of examples by name artists as is done in many other crafts. Some individuals may prefer to collect only the older dolls where others may gather any that appeal to them. Quite simply the choice of kachina dolls is too broad, too individualistic and changing to make a complete collection.

For the collector who wants to start a kachina doll collection, there are a few simple rules that will aid in sifting through the profusion of dolls.

1. Decide what you want to collect. A decision to collect only one category such as clowns will give finite limits to the collection and direction to the manner in which it is pursued.

2. Check for good carving. Good carving is characterized by proper body proportions and the correct relationship of upper leg or arm to the lower part of the limb. Feet and heads should be of the proper size and correctly placed. Details should be finished and the surface smoothed with no evidence of cracks or bad wood.

3. Determine the material. The doll should be lightweight if made of cottonwood. If it is extremely light and dents with a slight pressure of the fingernail it is made of balsa wood and is not a good doll. Very heavy dolls are made of pine, cottonwood limbs and other substitutes. Zuñi dolls are made of pine and not cottonwood root.

4. Check the painting. Lines and areas of color should be precise with firm straight edges and careful attention to detail. A highly sprayed or glossy surface is a distraction, but neither should the paint smudge with handling. The better the delineation of details such as costume and symbols the finer the doll.

5. Examine the paraphernalia. The gear that a doll wears or carries may be carved, painted or purchased but it should be present. Very few dolls are empty handed or show a bare neck from the lack of a ruff. Elements that are too gaudy such as dyed chicken feathers detract from the doll. *Note:* Hopi will use whatever materials are available to them and the choice is often one of expediency.

6. Accuracy. This is one of the most difficult areas for the collector. Bear in mind that *all* kachina dolls have not been photographed or described here. Dolls vary from village to village and change with the passage of time. Just as old dolls may be dropped from the repertoire new ones are added, and because a doll does not fit a picture does not mean that it is incorrect. Know the literature and be aware of variations.

7. How to identify a doll. Establishing the name, maker and village of a doll is important to the dealer and collector alike. However it is not an easy task, and too often the dealer may not have sufficient time for it. The collector should not depend entirely on the dealer but should, through literature and other collections, familiarize himself with types and characteristics. *Note:* Keep in mind, should you be in contact with Hopi that many will label as incorrect a great number of the dolls that are not made in their own village or assign them to the eastern pueblos.

8. Selected Readings: There are a number of good publications of kachinas and kachina dolls to assist collectors. A few are listed below:

BUNZEL, RUTH L. *Zuñi Katcinas*. Bureau of American Ethnology, Annual Report 47. Washington, D.C. 1929–30.
Many illustrations in black and white and color with lengthy descriptions and associated folk tales.

COLTON, HAROLD S. *Hopi Kachina Dolls with a Key to Their Identification*. University of New Mexico Press. Albuquerque, New Mexico. 1959.
The book contains a key to aid in the identification of kachinas, and most kachinas are identified by the numbers used in this publication. Although the author states that it is not complete it is an excellent reference for the majority of known dolls.

DOCKSTADER, FREDERICK J. *The Kachina and the White Man*. Cranbrook Institute of Science, Bull. 35. Bloomfield, Michigan. 1954.
An historical perspective of Hopi contact with non-Hopi and its influence on both dolls and kachinas.

EARLE, EDWIN and KENNARD, EDWARD A. *Hopi Kachinas*. J. J. Augustin. New York, New York. 1938.
A résumé of kachina ceremonies and dances of Third Mesa. Contains a number of excellent color plates of kachinas.

FEWKES, J. WALTER. *Tusayan Kachinas*. Bureau of American Ethnology, 15th Annual Report. Washington, D.C. 1897.
A preliminary study of the kachinas of First Mesa.

————. *Hopi Kachinas*. Bureau of American Ethnology, 21st Annual Report. Washington, D.C. 1903.
Many illustrations by Hopi artists of First Mesa kachinas. Widely copied by Hopi doll makers, it presents a specific time and mesa cluster of kachinas.

WRIGHT, BARTON A. *This is a Hopi Kachina*. Museum of Northern Arizona, Northland Press. 1965.
An introduction to kachina dolls for the beginner or the casually interested. Some color plates.
————. *Kachinas, a Hopi Artist's Documentary*. Heard Museum, Northland Press. Phoenix, Arizona. 1973.

A Hopi artist's rendering of kachinas derived from personal experience, publications and other Hopi. Over 200 color plates with explanations.

—————. *Kachinas, The Barry Goldwater Collection at the Heard Museum*. Heard Museum, W. A. Krueger Co. Phoenix, Arizona. 1975. One man's collection of kachina dolls with descriptions.

Explanatory Statement

IN ORDER TO SUB-DIVIDE the great mass of kachina dolls into more comprehensible units an effort has been made to group them by function. However, the separation of kachinas into classes is to a great extent an artificial system. As one student of the Hopi observed, "While any Hopi can describe in detail the costumes, songs, dance steps of a great number of kachinas, he remains comfortably vague on the subject of their relation to the forces of the universe, the nature of their power and the fate of the soul after death. Frequently members of other cult groups hold beliefs at variance with those of the kachina cult." To this could be added a note that it is not infrequent to have individuals, who because of their age, clan or society affiliations, are totally unaware of kachina functions, associations or purpose. He continues, "There is no tendency to develop a unified concept of the universe, to identify specific deities of their mythology with natural forces nor to arrange them in hierarchical system" (Kennard, 1938, p. 5). Nevertheless the Hopi, particularly the elders, do recognize groups of kachinas by their functions and while they would not consciously divide them in this manner it is possible to make and use such a categorization. Colton (1959, pp. 7–8) makes such an effort and isolates the following six classes, based on function as well as indicating other methods of classification. Additionally he recognizes another class of beings which he calls deities but does not include them in his class structure. Some of these deities have kachina forms and others do not. A few deities have more than one kachina form. Colton's classes are:

1. Chiefs: Those who take part in nine-day ceremonies.
2. Clowns: Those who offer comic relief during the dances.
3. Runners: Those who race with the men during the spring dances.

4. Kachinas that appear in the Bean Ceremony or *Powamu* of February and the Mixed Dances of spring.
5. The kachinas that are accompanied by manas who appear during the one-day dances.
6. Women kachinas, impersonated by men, who appear with other kachinas.

In addition he points out that there are several ill-defined sub-classes, some based on appearance such as the *kuwan* or brightly colored kachinas; *kwivi* the proud or heavily ornamented kachinas, and the functional group of *rügan* or rasping kachinas. This latter group are those appearing with female kachinas who accompany their songs with a musical instrument consisting of a notched stick placed across a resonating gourd. A sheep scapula or similar device that is scraped over the notched board produces a rhythmic sound. To these could be added other sub-classes such as the kachinas that are accompanied by drumming or those that wear lightning on their heads. There are many divisions of this nature used by the Hopi depending on context. The classes presented in this publication are in part those recognized by the Hopi and in part those arbitrarily imposed to lump similar forms of kachinas with Hopi associative clusters. These classes are not restrictive, and it is possible to have a single kachina that will belong to several classes because of varied functions. A kachina may thus be a guard, a chief kachina and an animal at one and the same time.

Chief Kachinas or Mongwi Kachinum

BOTH HOPI AND NON-HOPI recognize the Chief Kachinas as the most clearly defined class of spirits, possibly even more so than the deities, as they have a closer affinity to the clans. A Chief Kachina is a supernatural that belongs solely to a particular clan or related clans. The kachina can only be personated by a specific person within the kinship group and usually appears during the important nine–day ceremonies and never in the common plaza dances. There are, of course, exceptions to this generalization. The masks and costumes used to personify these kachinas may be refurbished from time to time but are never changed. They are considered sacrosanct and are kept by the clan matriarch to be guarded lest their potency be unwittingly wasted or the unwary be exposed to their power. They are cared for as persons and "fed" prayer meal at regular intervals. Each has specific functions which in essence are clan obligations to the Hopi as a group. Possibly the best characterization of them is that of a supernatural partner whose interests and actions are for the benefit of a specific clan. In addition they possess functions and powers which may be meshed with other chief kachinas to form an interlocking whole functioning for the benefit of the entire village.

The term Chief Kachina is perhaps an unfortunate choice in that it refers to their importance rather than a political position, but is nevertheless the accepted translation of Mongwi Kachinum. The Hopi term for these spirits is *wuya* and is in reference to a state of wisdom and power comparable to that of a religious elder in the real world.

In the Hopi elders resided traditional wisdom of both how the Hopi were to deal with the normal world and its attendant dangers and how to interact with the supernaturals. It was thus a simple matter to attribute to the Underworld a similar order of beings, with the *wuya* having more than passing interest in the affairs of the Hopi people and their clan leaders.

ANGWUSNASOMTAKA or TUMAS
Crow Mother, Man with Crow Wings Tied To

Angwusnasomtaka is the mother of the Hú or Whipper Kachinas and is considered by many Hopi to also be the mother of all kachinas. She appears during the Powamu or Bean Dance on all three mesas. However, on Third Mesa she is called Angwushahai-i, or Crow Bride, probably because she talks or sings, and comes dressed entirely in white. During the Powamu she supervises the initiation of the children into the Kachina Cult and carries the yucca whips with which they are struck by the Hú Kachinas. Later in the same ceremony she leads other kachinas into the village bearing in her arms a basket of corn kernels and bean sprouts to symbolically start the new season properly. This ceremony varies considerably from one mesa to another although the dolls do not. Kachina dolls of the Crow Mother abound in collections made twenty to thirty years ago but are not as commonly made today.

MASTOP
Death Fly Kachina

Mastop is present only on Third Mesa, arriving on the next to the last day of the Soyal Ceremony. This kachina always comes as a pair although they have not visited Old Oraibi for many decades. They represented a prayer for the fertility of the Hopi women from the dead Hopi ancestors. They arrive out of the northwest bounding about and beating the dogs with the short black- and white-striped sticks that they normally carry. They cavort about the village alternating this frenetic activity with short dashes into the crowds to grasp any age of

KEY TO COLOR PLATE 1
Hopi Name, English, (Colton #)

A. Angwusnasomtaka, Tumas, *Crow Mother, Man with Crow Wings tied to,* (12)
B. Mastop, *Death Fly Kachina,* (6)
C. Aholi, *Kachina Chief's Lieutenant,* (8)
D. Masau'u, *Earth God,* (D2)
E. Chakwaina, *No English translation,* (160)
F. Eototo, *Kachina Chief,* (7)

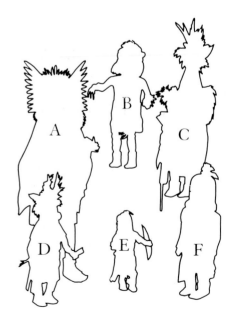

female by the shoulders from behind. By giving a series of short hops they imitate copulation and then return to their antics. This action is a serious fertility rite. Although a number of these dolls are made each year they are often confused with Matya, the Hand Kachina, and the wrong gear placed on the doll. Possibly because they have not been seen for so many years few of these dolls have all of the proper accoutrements.

AHOLI
Kachina Chief's Lieutenant

Aholi is the companion of Eototo during Powamu and aids him in the task of bringing moisture to the village. While Eototo is present on all three mesas, Aholi occurs only on Third Mesa. He is a beautiful kachina, and on the back of his many-colored cloak is painted a likeness of Muyingwa, one of the Germ Gods responsible for the germination of seeds. He is the *wuya* of the Pikyas or Young Corn Clan who care for the seed corn. The colors on his cloak are said to represent the flowers and brightness of summer. Legend has it that these two kachinas were partners ages ago in a different land. Aholi stayed behind and had his throat cut to allow Eototo time to escape as leader. After many lengthy migrations the two again met (in the guise of other men) and were reunited at Old Oraibi. Aholi and Eototo are supposed to always come as a pair. However, until a couple of decades ago Aholi was not carved at all or so infrequently that he is seldom represented in collections. Carved by Jimmie Kewanwytewa.

KEY TO COLOR PLATE 2
  Hopi Name, *English,* (Colton #)

A. Wupamo, *Long-billed Kachina,* (41)
B. Soyal, *Solstice or Return Kachina,* (1)
C. Hú, Tungwup, *Whipper Kachina,* (14)
D. Ahöla, Ahul, Mong, *Germ God, Chief Kachina, Solstice Kachina,* (2)

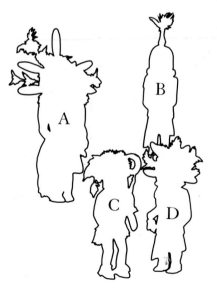

MASAU'U
Earth God

Masau'u is the deity who controls both the surface of the earth and the Underworld. In his capacity as ruler of the surface of the earth, he gave the Hopi their lands and bade them honor him with prayer plumes when they traveled the land. As god of death he controls the passage of the dead into the Underworld and the movement of the kachinas emerging from the netherland into the world of the living through the kivas. When he comes as a kachina he brings the most ancient of foods to the young men lest they forget what the old times were like. Masau'u is the only kachina that may appear during the closed season as he is the opposite of all living things. He may enter a kiva facing backward or even speak in reverse. He sometimes appears not as a kachina but as a handsome young man heavily ornamented but recognizable by his enormous feet. Masau'u is the *wuya* of the Masau'u Clan. His doll is often made and is well represented in many collections.

CHAKWAINA
No English translation

Chakwaina is a kachina brought to First Mesa from Zuñi by the Asa or Tansy Mustard Clan when they came to Sichomovi. From First Mesa the kachina was adopted on the other mesas. It has been said that Chakwaina represents Esteban the Moor, who led Marcos de Niza on the search for the Seven Cities of Cibola and who was reputedly killed at Zuñi for some transgression. However, Chakwaina is found in the Keresan and Tanoan pueblos along the Rio Grande as well and seems to have spread westward with the migration of the Asa Clan. Chakwaina, who is the *wuya* of this clan, is a warrior of great repute and his costume indicates this with its double bandoleers, buckskin kilt and the two warrior *pahos* or *huzrunkwa* on his head. The Chakwaina personation has a number of relatives, for there is a Chakwaina Grandmother, Mother and Sister, as well as a side dancer or Uncle. The doll is frequently made.

EOTOTO
Kachina Chief

Eototo is the chief of all kachinas and knows all of the ceremonies. He is the spiritual counterpart of the village chief and as such is called "father" of the kachinas. He controls the seasons and is sometimes called the husband of Hahai-i Wuhti. During the Powamu or Bean Dance on Third Mesa he conducts an elaborate ceremony with his companion or lieutenant, Aholi. He draws cloud symbols in corn flour on the ground pointing into the village. Aholi places his ceremonial staff on these and roars out his call. Then they both proceed onward toward the village. This is designed to draw the clouds and moisture into the pueblo. On First and Second Mesas Eototo is not accompanied by Aholi. Because of his knowledge of all of the ceremonies he appears in the Niman as well and apparently may be seen in any ceremony. His appearance is characteristic of many of the older kachinas in its simplicity. Minute differences like the presence or absence of ears mark the mesa differences in this kachina. This kachina belongs to the Bear Clan who are the traditional village chiefs. Carved by Jimmie Kewanwytewa.

WUPAMO
Long-Billed Kachina

Wupamo is both a chief kachina and a guard. Although he appears primarily as a guard during the Bean Dance he may serve in this same capacity at secret ceremonies in the kivas or assist with the cleaning of the springs by keeping the men on the job. During Powamu he may be seen patrolling the procession to keep the onlookers clear of the route or urging the laggard clowns onward. Moving quickly from place to place he uses yucca whips to threaten all offenders. For those who wish to be cured of rheumatism and approach him with that portion of their body turned in his direction, he will strike them several hard blows on the offending parts. This is considered a cure. This doll is often made by the Hopi with great variation in the symbolism on the face.

SOYAL KACHINA
The Solstice or Return Kachina

The Soyal Kachina is limited to Third Mesa although there are Solstice or Return Kachinas on the other mesas. No kachinas are to be seen on the Hopi mesas from the close of the Niman ceremony at the end of July until this kachina returns in late December. His reappearance signals the beginning of a new kachina season. He tours through the village placing prayer feathers or *pahos* at each kiva. These prayer offerings open the way for other kachinas to return to the village from the spirit world. He is believed to have taught the Hopi the art of making these *pahos*. Unfortunately the Soyal Kachina has not visited Third Mesa in over seventy years yet his small effigy is still occasionally made. The Soyal Kachina is one of the *wuya* of the Bear Clan. Carved by Jimmie Kewanwytewa.

HÚ KACHINA or TUNGWUP KACHINA
Whipper Kachina

The Hú Kachinas appear before the actual Bean Dance Parade to initiate the children into the Kachina Cult. They always come as a pair and accompany the Crow Mother who holds their whips for them. Many kachinas may receive the name of whipper because as guards they carry whips or because they whip for rheumatism. However, these are the only kachinas who whip for initiation. As each child is brought forward to stand before them they strike four solid blows across their backs with the yucca whips, taking turns at the task until all have received this treatment. When the chore is completed they whip each other and then the Crow Mother before disappearing from the kiva. This kachina does not appear very often as a doll. Carved by Jimmie Kewanwytewa.

AHÖLA, AHUL KACHINA or MONG KACHINA
The Germ God or Chief Kachina

Ahöla is said to represent Alosaka, one of the Germ Gods who control the growth and reproduction of all things. He is the Solstice or Return Kachina for First and Second Mesas as well as being a Sun Kachina. The women place corn ears in the kiva with him the day before he emerges in order that the corn will become a stronger seed and help in producing an abundance of corn. These ears are returned to the women when he emerges from the kiva with a single mana to assist him on Second Mesa, or two to help him on First Mesa. He visits each of the kivas to open it for the return of the kachinas after their long absence. His route also takes him to all of the clan houses in the village to strengthen them for the coming year. Before he departs he offers up prayers to the Sun for a long life, happiness and health and abundant crops for all of the people. Dolls of Ahöla are quite popular and are almost always found in larger collections. Carved by Jimmie Kewanwytewa.

Additional Chief Kachinas

Ahulani
Ahöla Mana
Akush
Alosaka
Angwushahai-i
Chaveyo
Chimon Mana
Chiwap
Danik'china
Hahai-i Wuhti
He-e-e
Huruing Wuhti
Kalavi
Kaletaka
Ketowa Bisena
Köchaf
Kököle
Kokosori
Kokyang Wuhti
Kwasai Taka
Lemowa
Maswik
Muyingwa
Nakiachop
Nataska
Ongchomo
Pachavu Hú
Patung
Pohaha
Saviki
Pöökonghoya
Shalako Taka
Shalako Mana
Söhönasomtaka
Tiwenu
Toho
Tokoch
Tsitoto
Tukwinong
Tukwinong Mana
Tumoala
Ursisimu
We-u-u
Wukokala
Wupa-ala
Wuyak-kuita
Yowe

Guard Kachinas or Tuwalakum

THIS CATEGORY of kachinas may be called either guards or warriors. When they appear individually they function more as sergeants-at-arms or policemen. In this role they either enforce an action such as the communal cleaning of springs or as a guard to prevent the approach of anyone or anything to the proximity of a location or ceremony. However, with the passing of years many of these functions have been lost as springs are converted to water systems and trails or roads become the province of highway departments. When they appear as a group such as in the Powamu Procession or during Pachavu times they are functioning as warriors. They surround the more sacred kachinas as a small but ferocious army of fearsome creatures. From these actions comes their name Ichivota or Angry Kachinas or as they are often called, the Watching Kachinas.

Many of the Guard Kachinas carry yucca whips which are indicative of their roles as warriors, protectors, and overseers. In some instances, such as with the fearsome warrior Hé-é-e, the Guards may serve to protect certain ceremonies from the potency of other kachinas.

KEY TO COLOR PLATE 3
Hopi Name, *English,* (Colton #)

A. Heoto, *no English translation,* (—)
B. Hólolo, *no English translation,* (103)
C. Hé-é-e, He Wuhti, *Warrior Woman,* (21)
D. Wuyak-kuita, *Broad-Faced Kachina,* (22)
E. Sipikne, many other names, *Zuñi Warrior God,* (152)

HEOTO KACHINA
No English translation

Heoto is a related form of the Chakwaina Kachinas that has appeared in comparatively recent times on the Hopi mesas. From the appearance this kachina was probably inspired from Zuñi. His function is that of a guard during the Bean Dance Parade and during Initiation years at the Pachavu Ceremony. Frequently he appears during the Kiva Dances as well as the Plaza Dances. His doll is often made nowadays but is rare in the older collections.

HÓLOLO
Wupa Nakava Kachina or Big Ears Kachina
Muyao Kachina or Moon Kachina

This kachina comes in two distinct forms both of which are called Hólolo, although each has a separate name as well as appearance. They take their name from the sound of their song. Hólolo appears as a line dancer in the Plaza Dances or in performances in the kiva and yet it is possible to find him as one of Hé-é-e's horde in the Bean Dance procession. Undoubtedly the latter is a minor function for the Hólolo. The illustrated kachina with the crescents on its face is the form called Muyao. The other form has enormous ears covered with many colored spots and is called Wupa Nakava. The Third Mesa Hopi claim that they originated this kachina and then it spread to the other villages. The kachina is not too often carved as it does not sell well.

KEY TO COLOR PLATE 4
Hopi Name, *English,* (Colton #)

A. Toho, *Mountain Lion Kachina,* (85)
B. Nakiachop, Akush, Shalako Warrior, *Silent Warrior, Ladder Dancer,* (—)
C. Hilili, Powak'china, *Witch Kachina,* (185)
D. Sakwa Hú, *Blue Whipper,* (—)
E. Ewiro, *Warrior Kachina,* (202)

40

HÉ-É-E or HE WUHTI
Warrior Woman

Hé-é-e is a kachina who represents a warrior spirit. It is either a man dressed in women's clothes or a woman using men's equipment depending on the mesa where one hears the story. At Second Mesa the story goes: a young man changed clothes with his bride in a corn field and was only half-dressed with his hair up in a whorl on one side and loose on the other and with his pants on under the dress when he saw enemies approaching. Grabbing his weapons he fought them off until assistance arrived. At Oraibi it is a young woman having her hair put up who takes up her father's weapons till help arrives. Despite the variation in the folktales the kachina is a potent warrior, and during the Pachavu Ceremony she leads a band of fearsome warrior kachinas to protect the procession. Because she is so potent there are other guards who protect certain ceremonies from her dangerous presence. As a doll she is carved with regularity and can be usually be found in any contemporary collection.

WUYAK-KUITA
Broad-Faced Kachina

The Broad-Faced Kachina is the most typical form of guard, as he appears in the Bean Dance on all three mesas. On First Mesa he comes with the Soyoko during the Powamu, while on the Second and Third he guards the procession during Bean Dance ceremony. He brings up the rear and keeps everyone moving forward together. On Third Mesa he also prevents one of the other kachinas, Hé-é-e, from approaching too closely during the Palölökong or Water Serpent ceremony when it is being held in the kivas. Carrying a yucca whip in either hand this kachina moves with a heavy, ponderous gait as though little exists to give him pause. Usually the dolls carved of him show this solidity in their carving. Carvings of Wuyak-kuita appear with regularity but not in any great quantity. Carved by Jackson Seckletstewa.

SIPIKNE, TALAMOPAIYAKYA, MOPAIYAKYA, TALAIMOCHOVI, SALIMBIYE, SALIMOPIA, SALIMOPAIYAKYA
Zuñi Warrior Kachina

This kachina, an import from Zuñi, is undergoing a gradual transformation into a more Hopi form of kachina through slight innovations which change the original figure. Formerly the Sipikne came with no rattles at all and danced

42

furiously in complete silence, but of recent sleigh bells have been added to his costume. He comes in all of the directional colors and is a favorite of the kachina carvers. The kachina is characterized by such rapid movement when he appears in a dance or as a guard that only the younger men can maintain the pace. The multiple names of this kachina are derived from variations on the Zuñi name of Salimopaiyakya or the fact that he has a long snout, Talaimochovi. His effigy is easy to carve and yet colorful.

TOHO
Mountain Lion Kachina

The Toho or Mountain Lion Kachina often accompanies such animals as the Deer or Antelope Kachinas when they appear in the Line Dances of spring. However, during the Pachavu or Tribal Initiation about every fourth year Toho appears as a guard. Armed with yucca whips he patrols the procession in company with Hé-é-e and the other warrior or guard kachinas. Toho is a favorite doll at the present time whereas five years ago or longer the doll was rarely carved. It is almost always carved as an action doll.

NAKIACHOP, AKUSH
The Silent Warrior, Shalako Warrior

Nakiachop is probably one of a generic group known as the Dawn or Morning Kachinas. He is almost identical with Talavai-i, the best known of these kachinas. He appears in the January Pamuya as the Silent Warrior or Akush. He is purported to be the Ladder Dance (Sakti) Kachina of antiquity. These kachinas showed great bravery in climbing to the top of long poles set in sockets at the mesa edge and then swinging the tree tips out over the drop-off or leaping from one tree to another. Dolls of this kachina are extremely rare as so few carvers know or have seen the kachina.

HILILI, POWAK'CHINA
No English Translation, Witch Kachina

This kachina came from Zuñi to the Hopi but had arrived in the former location from Acoma or Laguna. In those pueblos he is known as Heleleka. When Hilili first appeared he was known as the Powak or Witch Kachina and was regarded with great suspicion. This often occurs with a kachina newly introduced from another pueblo, particularly when it is a fearsome kachina. The women still shudder and draw back whenever he appears. Nowadays he is used as a guard at Powamu and may also appear in the Kiva or Plaza Dances.

43

There is a wide variety of these kachinas, some are marked by the encircled or staring eyes, or a diagonally divided mask. Others are recognized by the elaborate cross piece on the head and nearly always by a wildcat skin draped across the shoulders. Kachina carvers delight in making this doll and elaborating on the appearance although they made even more a few years ago. Carved by Henry Shelton.

SAKWA HÚ
Blue Whipper Kachina

Sakwa Hú is reportedly an old kachina and yet it appears in none of the older collections. Despite this lack the Hopi who were asked unanimously agreed that it was a very old kachina. This anomaly is probably due to a change in the appearance of the kachina and a continuation of the name. It is most often impersonated by one of the smaller or younger boys during the Powamu. Sakwa Hú serves as a guard of this procession on Third Mesa. The doll has become quite a favorite of Third Mesa carvers during recent years. Carved by Wilbert Talashoma.

EWIRO
Warrior Kachina

Ewiro is an old type of Third Mesa Kachina who resembles Chakwaina's Sister on Second Mesa. He formerly appeared as a sergeant-at-arms to keep the men at the task of cleaning the springs or other village chores. Occasionally nowadays he is used as a warrior against the clowns but most often he is seen as a guard during the Powamu and Pachavu ceremonies. Dolls of this kachina are very rare. This one was made in the 1930s. Carved by Jimmie Kewanwytewa.

ADDITIONAL GUARDS

Ahote	Kaletaka	Nangasohu	Sohu
Chakwaina	Kipok	Palakwayo	Tokoch
Chaveyo	Komanchi	Pohaha	Tungwup Taha-um
Holi	Mongwu	Sikyachan' Taka	Tuskiapaya
Ho-óte	Monongya	Sio Hemis Taha-um	Wupamo
Hototo	Motsin	Söhönasomtaka	Yowe

Ogres or Sosoyok't

THE OGRES are disciplinary kachinas who come to the villages on First and Second Mesa either during the Powamu Ceremony or immediately thereafter. Formerly they also came to Old Oraibi on Third Mesa but this ceremony fell into disuse sometime in the early 1900s.

About a week before the Soyoko are to appear either Soyok' Wuhti or Soyok Mana and an attendant monster appear and go through the village pausing at each house. The Soyoko or Ogre Woman tells the younger children that they must catch mice or grind corn against the time when she will return. To each boy she gives a yucca snare and tells him to catch mice. To each girl she gives corn and warns her to grind it well, for if she returns and finds no cornmeal or mice she will take the children for food instead.

A week later she returns with a great troup of ugly kachinas, each a monster and some of whom are carrying baskets on their backs with which to haul away the youngsters. Approaching a house, the Ogres demand meat, and the small trapper of mice or grinder of corn must then proffer his meager ransom to the growling, stamping crew. Regardless of what is offered it is indignantly refused and more food demanded lest they take the child. To add weight to their demands they recount the misbehavior of the children, telling how they do not mind and are no help to their parents. Any petty misdeed that is brought up is countered by a relative who points out that the child has really learned his lesson and no longer makes such mistakes. They then offer other food to the monsters in place of the children. Eventually the monsters go clacking and grumbling away to pile their food in some kiva. At the end of the day the men of the village lure the Ogres into a dance on some pretext, and then while the creatures are thoroughly involved in learning the dance the men suddenly leap upon them and wrest from them all of their ill-gotten gains. Deprived of everything they are driven from the village.

The children who are involved at every step learn a series of object lessons. They must contribute to the food supply or die. Their well-being is dependent on the good will of their relatives and also that the village men will protect its inhabitants.

WIHARU
White Ogre or White Nataska

Wiharu is merely a white version of the Black Nataska. He carries a saw as well as a bow and arrows for hunting. Probably these kachinas came in all colors at one time for there is a Blue Nataska mask in existence. He stands with the other Nataskas, stamping and clacking his beak as they await their food or the chance for a child.

CHAVEYO
The Giant Kachina

Chaveyo is a threatening kachina who may appear at anytime in the spring when the youngsters are bad to dispense disciplinary action. He may threaten adults who misbehave as well. If the men, for example, are remiss in their ceremonial duties it is Chaveyo who may speed them on their way. During a recent crisis when members of an ethnic minority were attempting a demonstration on Second Mesa, it was Chaveyo who came to force them to leave. Chaveyo occurs in virtually every pueblo from the Hopi in the west to the San Juan in the east and in each village he performs the same role. He is often seen with the Soyoko of First Mesa assisting them in their role.

KEY TO COLOR PLATE 5
Hopi Name, *English*, (Colton #)

A. Wiharu, *White Ogre, White Nataska,* (31)
B. Chaveyo, *Giant Kachina,* (37)
C. Owanga-zrozro, *Mad or Stone-eater Kachina,* (198)
D. Sikya Heheya, *Yellow Heheya,* (—)
E. Toson Koyemsi, *Sweet Cornmeal Tasting Mudhead or Mudhead Ogre,* (32)

46

OWANGA-ZROZRO
The Mad or Stone-Eater Kachina

Although this kachina is a monster or an ogre it is not one of the Sosoyok' t. Appearing instead during the Powamu, it fussily attacks the smaller Koyemsi who constantly bedevil him. He varies greatly from mesa to mesa in appearance but not in actions. He is so ill-tempered that he eats rocks in frustration and anger. He is included with the ogres because of his interaction with the smaller Koyemsi. The doll is an older form of carving having the barely indicated hands and feet of dolls made in the 1920s.

SIKYA HEHEYA
The Yellow Heheya

Yellow Heheyas belong to Second Mesa and are the Ogres' main helpers in those villages. They carry ropes to threaten the children or to lasso the unwary onlooker. As the food is gathered in the village throughout the day they carry it back to the kiva where it is stored until evening. During the dance in the evening these kachinas behave in a lewd and lecherous manner until batted into line by Soyok' Mana. Oddly enough the dolls are not often carved although a similar kachina on Third Mesa, Toson Heheya, appears quite often.

TOSON KOYEMSI
Sweet Cornmeal Tasting Mudhead or Mudhead Ogre

These kachinas accompany the true ogres and are asked to sample the cornmeal ground by the little girls and determine its value. They make a long process of determining whether the sweet cornmeal is indeed good or whether the Ogres

KEY TO COLOR PLATE 6
Hopi Name, *English,* (Colton #)

A. Motsin, *Disheveled Kachina,* (254)

B. Kuwan Powamu Koyemsi, *Colored Bean Dance Mudhead,* (—)

C. Sio Hemis Hú, *Zuñi Hemis Whipper,* (—)

D. Awatovi Soyok' Taka, *Awatovi Ogre Man,* (26)

E. Soyoko, Soyok' Wuhti, *Ogre Woman,* (24)

48

should take the girl. These same kachinas often appear at dawn on the last day of the Powamu Ceremony to deliver bean sprouts and presents to the children. Thus they belong to another class, that of the Talavai or Dawn Kachinas. This doll is dressed as he appears as attendant to the Soyoko when she notifies the children on Second Mesa.

MOTSIN
The Dishevelled Kachina

Motsin is primarily a guard or sergeant-at-arms who enforces participation on community projects. He can, however, be used in the vanguard of the Sosoyok' t. He carries a quirt to enforce his demands and a rope to lead the recalcitrant to work. This doll is characteristic of the recent action dolls in the detail of the carving. Carved by Carl Sulu.

KUWAN POWAMU KOYEMSI
The Colored Bean Dance Mudhead

A Powamu Koyemsi may accompany the Ogres on their warning circuit through the village. The marks on his forehead indicate that he is one of the Toson Koyemsi who will later taste the girls' cornmeal. This doll and the Toson Koyemsi indicate how divergent costumes can be on the same type of kachina.

SIO HEMIS HÚ
Zuñi Hemis Whipper

The Zuñi Hemis Whipper is an uncle or side dancer for the Sio Hemis Kachinas. It can appear with the Sosoyok' t on rare occasions but is usually to be found in the Bean Dance procession or the Mixed Kachina Dance. This small doll is characteristic of the smaller or miniature dolls being made by carvers like Mary Shelton. Carved by Rousseau Roy.

AWATOVI SOYOK'TAKA
Awatovi Ogre Man

This ogre is an import from the village of Awatovi, destroyed early in the 1700s and the survivors taken to the Hopi villages of today. The Awatovi Soyok' Taka behaves almost exactly like the Wiharu or White Nataska and is probably a variant of that kachina. The Soyok' Taka stands at the side during the ordeal of the children, stamping and grumbling, with a large basket ready and waiting on its back.

SOYOKO, or SOYOK'WUHTI
Ogre Woman

Soyok' Wuhti is the Ogre Woman of First Mesa who appears after or during the Powamu and asks the children to hunt or grind for her and threatens to eat them if they do not. When she reappears with all of the monsters her arms are bloodstained and she carries a long crook for catching children, as well as a huge blood-stained knife. She pauses from time to time to fling her stringy hair back from her staring eyes as she searches for some young child to eat. On Second Mesa she is content to stand to one side shuffling about as the other monsters do while Soyok' Mana, a related kachina that accompanies the Soyok' Wuhti on First Mesa, demands food. Soyok' Wuhti, when she formerly came to Third Mesa, was quite different in appearance, with a long sharp beak and a red tongue hanging from the end of it. However, her behavior was the same as at the other mesas. On Second Mesa, Atosle, a related form, resembles Soyok' Wuhti more than on First Mesa where the Atosle is a male. Carved by Jimmie Kewanwytewa.

ADDITIONAL KACHINAS

Atosle	Nataska	Hahai-i Wuhti
Awatovi Soyok' Wuhti	Masau'u	Soyok' Mana
Kumbi Nataska	We-u-u	

Kachina Women or Momoyam

KACHINAS HAVE LIVES that are the same as any other Hopi, and consequently most of them have mothers, wives and sisters who accompany them when they are seen in ceremonies and dances. These female kachinas are impersonated by men with one exception, the Pachavuin Mana. In this one instance the impersonator is a woman. Other personages often resemble Momoyam or Kachina women but are not, instead they are social dancers or members of women's societies. The men who take the impersonation of the kachina women in ceremonies do so by personal choice or the general accord of their kiva mates. The decision is often based on the men's small size or simply because they do an excellent job of impersonation. There is never any onus attached to the role.

There is some degree of confusion among the younger men as to which personage they are carving, for all are crafted without regard to their roles. While the younger men may confuse Takursh Mana with Kachin' Mana, this is not true when dances or ceremonies demand the presence of women kachinas. Any kachina may have a mana for accompaniment and the kachin' mana simply takes their name. Thus when a kachin' mana accompanies a kachina such as Kahaila it becomes Kahaila Kachin' Mana.

KEY TO COLOR PLATE 7
  Hopi Name, *English,* (Colton #)

A. Nuvak'chin Mana, Köcha Kachin' Mana, *Snow Kachina Girl or White Kachina Girl,* (100)
B. Palhik' Mana, *Water Drinking Girl, Butterfly Girl,* (120)
C. Pachavuin Mana, *Harvest Girl,* (23)
D. Masau'u Kachin' Mana, *Death Kachina Girl,* (124)
E. Hahai-i Wuhti, *Pour Water Woman, Kachina Mother, Kachina Grandmother,* (44)

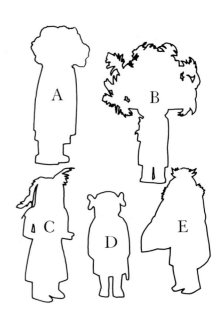

NUVAK'CHIN' MANA, KÖCHA KACHIN' MANA
Snow Kachina Girl, White Kachina Girl

This kachina girl is most often seen during the Niman Ceremony. She represents the snow and is one of the rasping or Rügan Kachinas as well. Her presence is a prayer for the coming cold weather that snow may fall and replenish the ground with moisture.

PALHIK' MANA, SHALAKO MANA, POLI MANA
Water Drinking Girl, Shalako Girl, Butterfly Girl

The Palhik' Mana is not a kachina but rather a woman's dance personage. Women who appear in the Mamzrau Initiation Dance are called the Palhik' Manas. They are never masked except on Third Mesa, although they all appear to be when carved as dolls. The Palhik' Mana is often called the Butterfly Kachina Girl, this is then confused with Poli Mana who is the real Butterfly Girl but not a kachina. Another form with which the Palhik' Mana is often interchanged is the kachina Shalako Mana. These two intergrade in appearance when carved as dolls thus adding more difficulties to identification. However, this does not seem to matter to the Hopi who treat them synonymously anyway. Despite the confusion the doll is one of the most beautiful carved by the Hopi and is a favorite subject.

PACHAVUIN MANA
Harvest Girl

The Pachavuin Mana is not a kachina, although she may appear in a mask. She may be either married or single, although she is called a girl. She is a society

KEY TO COLOR PLATE 8
Hopi Name, *English,* (Colton #)

A. Takursh Mana, Angak'chin Mana, *Yellow Corn Girl or Long-Haired Kachina Girl,* (129)
B. Hoho Mana, *Zuñi Kachina Girl,* (156)
C. Alo Mana, *no English translation,* (215)
D. Kachin' Mana, Hemis Kachin' Mana, *Kachina Girl, Hemis Kachina Girl,* (133)
E. Horo Mana, Masan Wuhti, Yohozro Wuhti, *Comb Hair Upwards Girl, or Cold Bringing Woman,* (101)

woman, one of four, who is performing the ceremonial duty of symbolically bringing food to the village during the Pachavu or Tribal Initiation Rites. The sole function of this mana is to carry an enormous load of bean sprouts from the shrine of Kowawaima to the village. This kachina doll is quite rare in any collection although they appear on all mesas. Carved by Jimmie Kewanwytewa.

MASAU'U KACHIN' MANA
Death Kachina Girl

When the Masau'u Kachina comes to dance in the plazas it is accompanied by a mana. Masau'u Mana is one of the rasping kachinas who uses a rasp and gourd resonator to accompany the songs of her male counterpart. Her face is covered with a gray-brown mud as she is supposed to bring heavy rains when she appears. This doll is uncommon but is being carved more often than formerly. Carved by Jimmie Kewanwytewa.

HAHAI-I WUHTI
Pour Water Woman, Kachina Mother, Kachina Grandmother

Hahai-i Wuhti is said to be the mother of all kachinas, as is the Crow Mother. The reference is to duty rather than actual blood relationship. She is also spoken of as the mother of dogs. Her real children are the monsters, the Nataskas, with Chaveyo as the father, although other Hopi say that her husband is Eototo and that she corresponds in a female role to his position. It is true that she is in many important ceremonies such as the Hopi Shalako, the Water Serpent and the Powamu. Hahai-i Wuhti is unusual in that she is quite vocal, a rarity among kachinas. Doll carvers make her effigy in the flat form to be the first present that a baby receives. These same dolls are also given to captive eagles. Later dolls in full relief are carved and given to the girls.

TAKURSH MANA, ANGAK'CHIN' MANA
Yellow Girl, Long-Haired Kachina Girl

This mana appears with many kachinas such as the Angak'china, Ma-alo, Pawik'china and others. They dance in a line separate from the kachinas but following the same pattern, turning and gesturing. They are also Rügan as they rasp an accompaniment for the male kachinas' songs. They are characterized by the red bangs and beard. Dolls of this kachin' mana are relatively common. Carved by Jimmie Kewanwytewa.

HOHO MANA
Zuñi Kachina Girl

This mana, who is an import from Zuñi, most often accompanies the Zuñi Hemis Kachina (Sio Hemis). The Kachin' Mana is unsure in its performance whether it is a maiden or a man and alternates its behavior between the two. One moment it may dance like a man and the next it behaves as a woman. The doll was formerly much more popular than today when it appears only occasionally. It is usually represented in some quantity in all of the older collections.

ALO MANA
No English translation

Alo Mana accompanies the Koroasta Kachina, Kahaila and others. It seems to have been introduced from the eastern pueblos which may account for its presence with kachinas from that area. Alo Mana behaves in the same manner as does the standard Hopi Kachin' Mana. The mana is not often seen as a doll nor is it in any of the older collections.

KACHIN' MANA
Kachina Girl, Yellow Corn Girl

This Kachin' Mana is the most ubiquitous of all the women who appear with other kachinas. She merely changes her name to that of the kachina with whom she is dancing although her appearance does not change. Thus she is one moment an Ahöla Mana and the next a Hemis Kachin' Mana or a Hokya Mana. Her presence is a prayer for corn. She is often called the Hemis Kachin' Mana for she appears most with that kachina. Many dolls are carved of this kachin' mana.

HORO MANA, MASAN WUHTI, YOHOZRO WUHTI
Comb Hair Upwards Girl, Motioning Woman, Cold-Bringing Woman

This Tewa Kachin' Mana usually appears during the Powamu on First Mesa. Her function is to bring the cold to the Hopi, just as does the Nuvak'chin' Mana. She is, in most instances, an alternate for the Köcha Kachin' Mana. She carries a Hopi hair brush and with it she musses people's hair much as does the winter wind. Dolls in her effigy are quite unusual. Carved by Jimmie Kewanwytewa.

A-ha Kachin' Mana
Ahöla Mana
Angwushahai-i
Atosle
Awatovi Ogre Woman
Butterfly Kachina Mana
Chakwaina Mana
Chakwaina Mother
Chakwaina Grandmother
Chimon Mana
Crow Mother

Hano or Hokyan Mana
Hé-é-e
Heheya Kachin' Mana
Huruing Wuhti
Kahaila Kachin' Mana
Kokopell Mana
Kokyang Wuhti
Konin Mana
Maswik'chin' Mana
Mong' Wuhti
Piptu' Wuhti

Pohaha
Poli Mana
Powamu So-aum
Sakwa Mana
Sakwats Mana
Shalako Mana
Söhönasomtaka
Soyok Mana
Soyoko
Tasap Kachin' Mana
Yunya Mana
and others

Mixed Kachinas or Sosoyohim Kachinum

THE HOPI EMPLOY a number of kachinas for cloud spirits as their interest is always in the production of moisture whether as rain or snow. It is consequently not surprising to find kachinas which range from the simple Thunder-Making Kachina to the far more complex Shalakos. Because virtually every kachina who dances is in one way or another a rain-bringing spirit in addition to its other attributes, many are not singled out as rain spirits.

Most of the kachinas who are a specific form of rain-bringer dance during the spring and summer months to assist the growing plants. Thus in the Mixed or Line Dances held in the plaza one finds a wide variety of these kachinas. The Shalako, whose performance follows the Niman at rare intervals, is the most divergent of these cloud people. The Hopi do not make this grouping of Soyohim Omau-u kachinas. Rather they are content to lump all Soyohim or Mixed Kachinas into one enormous stockpile from which they draw the needed spirits. These spirits may be insect, cloud, or other Indians, but all have one basic function: the bringing of rain.

If everyone is happy and the kachina impersonators are dancing, the village will be gay and colorful, the real kachina spirits will pause as they pass, and the rain will come to the thirsty fields and replenish the springs. If the people argue or are hostile to one another, rain will not come, as the supernaturals avoid unhappiness and anger. In belief of this sequence of events, the Hopi dress their gayest and have an open house that no visitor may be turned away hungry or angry and henceforth spoil the image of the village and offend the kachinas. While this is the Hopi feeling, it should not be considered as a carte blanche for every casual visitor to enter a home where he or she is not known and have a meal.

HAHAI-I WUHTI
Kachina Mother (see page 56)
Carved by Lowell Talashoma.

DANIK'CHINA
Cloud Guard Kachina

Four of these kachinas appear with the Hopi Shalako pair and serve as their uncles. Two dance with the Shalako Taka and two with the Shalako Mana. They carry long willow branches with which they periodically strike the ground raising little eddies of dust, much as the winds do around the base of the thunderheads in summer before it starts to rain. Effigies of this kachina are extremely rare because they appear only with the Hopi Shalakos who come at such infrequent intervals. Carved by Lowell Talashoma.

HOPI SHALAKO TAKA
Hopi Shalako Male

The Hopi Shalako is a figure that superficially resembles the Zuñi Shalako enough to have caused great confusion in the early writings. This kachina seems to represent all of the cloud people and behaves more as a deity than a kachina. He and the mana, flanked by the Tukwinong Kachinas and the Danik' chinas, are led into the plaza by Hahai-i Wuhti who positions them and indicates each move the Shalakos make. Because their costumes and head-gear repeat the theme of clouds over and over again it would seem that Hahai-i Wuhti is directing the clouds to pause over the Hopi villages. These personages

KEY TO COLOR PLATE 9
Hopi Name, *English,* (Colton #)

A. Hahai-i Wuhti, *Pour Water Woman, Kachina Mother, Kachina Grandmother,* (44)
B. Danik'china, *Cloud Guard Kachina,* (266)
C. Hopi Shalako Taka, *Hopi Cloud Man, Cloud Person Male,* (117)
D. Hopi Shalako Mana, *Hopi Cloud Girl, Cloud Person Female,* (118)
E. Tukwinong, *Cumulus Cloud Kachina,* (97)
F. Tukwinong Mana, *Cumulus Cloud Kachina Girl,* (98)

appear so rarely that they have come only four times in the last hundred years. Carved by Lowell Talashoma.

HOPI SHALAKO MANA
Hopi Shalako Girl

The Shalako Mana is almost identical with the Shalako Taka in appearance and is his counterpart in action. The mana is almost indistinguishable from her mate and can be told only by the white color of her boots, the red maiden's robe she wears, her white face and her square earrings. The narrow shoulderless figures of the Shalakos rising seven or eight feet above the plaza make strikingly beautiful dancers and the dolls echo that appearance. In recent years there has been a change from the carved or painted wooden feathers to real ones which simulate the necessary eagle plumage. Carved by Lowell Talashoma.

TUKWINONG
Cumulus Cloud Kachina

The Tukwinong Kachina may appear in the Soyohim dances but he is always present when the Hopi Shalakos come. His form varies a little between mesas but not enough to confuse his identity. On First Mesa he wears a mask with white cloud symbols on top and a white mask. On Second and Third Mesas his face is masked by hanging feathers which resemble falling rain below the white cloud symbols. He represents the deluges of rain which fall from the towering thunderheads, and may even be another aspect of Sotuknangu. The kachina carries a jug of water in each hand and is always barefoot. Carved by Lowell Talashoma.

KEY TO COLOR PLATE 10
Hopi Name, *English,* (Colton #)

A. Omau-u Kachina, *Cloud Kachina,* (—)
B. Nuvak'china, *Snow Kachina,* (99)
C. Umtoinaka, *Making-Thunder Kachina,* (237)
D. Sio Shalako, *Zuñi Cloud Person,* (158)
E. Sotuknangu, *Heart of the Sky God,* (D1)

TUKWINONG MANA
Cumulus Cloud Kachina Girl

The Tukwinong Mana who is the sister of the Tukwinong Kachina appears only during the Hopi Shalako ceremony. She holds a tray of cornmeal which is shaped into a rounded mound and then divided into four colors of meal to represent the directional colors, undoubtedly representing the clouds from the points of the compass. The mana's legs and hands are coated with the blue-gray of mud from the village spring. In this particular doll the carver has made her with a gourd resonator and rasp rather than the usual tray of cornmeal. Carved by Lowell Talashoma.

OMAU-U KACHINA
Cloud Kachina

The Omau-u Kachina formerly appeared in the Mixed Dances. For some reason this kachina has dropped in popularity since the early part of this century and is now virtually unknown. The doll appears only in the older collections. It appears to have been a kachina representing clouds in general and its form was widely variable.

NUVAK'CHINA
Snow Kachina

The Snow Kachina appears in many Hopi dances such as the Powamu, Kiva Dances, Water Serpent Ceremony, and Mixed Kachina Dances. He is very important on First Mesa. Presumably he lives on the top of the San Francisco Peaks and helps to bring the cold and the snows of winter to the Hopi. He has a close tie with the water in the springs of the various villages as the snow is the main replenisher of the springs. His image is often used by many non-Indian businesses as an advertising device.

UMTOINAKA
Making-Thunder Kachina

Making-Thunder Kachina is one of the great variety of kachinas that appear in the Mixed Plaza Dances of spring and early summer. He carries a bull-roarer which he uses to simulate the sound of thunder from time to time while he is dancing. He may on occasion serve also as a guard. Dolls of this kachina are not often made. A functionally related form is the Möna Kachina (236) who appears in the Mixed Dances on Third Mesa.

SIO SHALAKO
Zuñi Shalako

The Sio Shalako is an adaptation of a Zuñi kachina. Although its inspiration was from a Zuñi kachina it no longer behaves as one and should be considered as a separate personage. When it came to the Hopi first as a group of four kachinas sometime around 1850 it behaved very much as its counterpart in Zuñi. Since that time however it has changed until only one comes today, and it is accompanied by a Sio Shalako Mana. It appears during the Pamuya series in January on First Mesa but comes at other times as well. In addition it is found on all three mesas. The view of the nine foot high kachina is indeed a rare and beautiful sight. More dolls are made of the Sio Shalako than of the Hopi Shalako Taka but not of the Mana. Carved by Wilson Kaye.

SOTUKNANGU
Heart of the Sky God

This individual is a deity and is impersonated by the religious elders in certain kiva ceremonies. In addition it has a kachina form which may appear during the Powamu or on all mesas in the Mixed Dances of springtime. The deity is believed to control the dangerous thunderheads, lightning and destructive rain. He is an indomitable warrior and his symbol is the morning star. When he appears in the Soyohim or Mixed Dance he wears a peaked hat indicative of the towering thunderheads, and he carries in his hands the expandable crossed sticks which represent lightning. Although he is the embodiment of the destructive forces within thunderheads, some Christianized Hopi have equated him with the Christian Deity.

ADDITIONAL CLOUD KACHINAS

Hail Kachina
Kwinyao or North Wind Deity
Masau'u Mana
Möna or Thunder Kachina
Omau-u Wuhti or Cloud Woman

Saiastasana, the Zuñi Rain Priest
  of the North
Shalako Warrior
White Cloud Clown
Yaponcha, the Wind Deity

Indian Kachinas or Sosoyohim Yotam Kachinum

THE HOPI HAVE CONVERTED many of their neighbors into kachinas. These kachinas are not borrowed from these groups but are instead figures who represent that tribe of Indians. The Kachina is believed to be the essence of the people and in no way a true representation of their actual appearance. Ethnologists speculate that this may have begun as an effort to capitalize on the luck or "power" the other tribes apparently possessed. Each of these Indian groups has an aspect that has been captured by the Hopi and incorporated into their kachina forms to produce a type. It may be the dress and pose of a Navajo Kachina Girl or the body paint of an Apache, but the result is a characterization. This "type" is much the same as our over-simplification of the humorless British, the French lover, or the stolid German. These kachinas have roles in many ceremonies or dances without any consideration of their ethnic overtones. They are most often, however, found in the position of uncles when occurring in the Mixed Dance or as groups in the Plaza Dances.

KEY TO COLOR PLATE 11
Hopi Name, *English,* (Colton #)

A. Tasap or Tasaf Kachina, *Navajo Kachina,* (137)

B. Tasap or Tasaf Kachin' Mana, *Navajo Kachina Girl,* (138)

C. Konin Kachina, *Havasupai Kachina,* (143)

D. Konin Kachin' Mana, *Havasupai Kachina Girl,* (—)

E. Komanshi Kachin' Mana, *Comanche Kachina Girl,* (—)

TASAP KACHINA
Navajo Kachina

The Tasap Kachina is the epitomization of the Navajo for the Hopi. This kachina bears a vague resemblance to the costume of Navajo dancers but otherwise resembles a bird more than another group of Indians. The kachinas dance in a line in the plaza in the spring. Their movements are rather slow as they dance but with a heavy beat. The Hopi are fond of this dance and it is frequently performed. The name of the kachina is often written in two different ways which are dialectic differences in the language. The people of Third Mesa end the word with a p and those of Second Mesa with an f, but the kachina remains the same. There are many kachinas of Navajo inspiration such as the Tasap Yeibichai, Tasap Naastadji, Mösa, Nihiyo and others.

TASAP KACHIN' MANA
Navajo Kachina Girl

The Tasap Kachin' Mana accompanies the male dancers in this well-liked dance. Their costume is that of the Navajo woman. The upthrust snout and tipped-back head are the mannerisms which the Hopi assert to be that of the Navajo women when dancing. The effigy of this kachina is often made, but seldom at the same time as its partner. This is unfortunate as they make a very nice set. Carved by Gene Kewenvoyouma.

KEY TO COLOR PLATE 12
Hopi Name, *English,* (Colton #)

A. Konin Taha-um, Kalampa, *Supai Uncle or Side Dancer,* (—)
B. Konin, *Cohonino,* (—)
C. Tiwenu, *Laguna—Santo Domingo?* (—)
D. Hano Mana, *Tewa Girl,* (264)
E. Siok'china, *Zuñi Kachina,* (262)

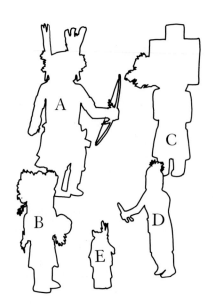

KONIN KACHINA, SUPAI KACHINA
Cohonino Kachina

KONIN KACHIN' MANA, SUPAI KACHIN' MANA
Cohonino Kachina Girl

This pair of kachinas are the characterizations of the Havasupai neighbors of the Hopi to the west. The colored faces presumably represent the style of face-painting used by this group many years ago. The girls are dressed in the buck-skins they formerly wore. Their appearance is similar to that of the social dancers who appear in the fall. These two dolls are by the same carver which is somewhat unusual as pairs are not often carved or sold at the same time. Carved by Gene Kewenvoyouma.

KOMANCHI KACHIN' MANA
Comanche Kachina Girl

The Comanche Kachina Girl is another of the social dance figures that is portrayed as a kachina. Most of these dolls such as the Konin and Konin Mana, Poli Mana and the Buffalo dancers have two forms, a social dance, or unmasked variety, and a masked, or kachina, impersonation. This is an antique doll made in the older style of carving with real hair added for the braids.

KONIN TAHA-UM, KONIN KACHINA, KALAMPA
Supai Kachina, Havasupai Uncle, Havasupai Side Dancer

These two dolls are characteristic of the development of kachinas. The first time the kachina appeared is unknown, but it became increasingly popular in the late 1950s, and as is characteristic with new kachinas it received multiple names. It was assigned to the Apache, Ute, Paiute, and finally the Havasupai. Nowadays it is generally recognized as another form of Havasupai kachina. The upper figure is painted more like an Apache kachina than the lower one but is obviously the same kachina. The "uncle" or side dancer is the one shown at the top holding a bow in his hand. The regular line dancer stands below him.

TIWENU
Laguna/Santo Domingo

Purportedly this kachina is derived from the eastern pueblos and represents one of these groups. Information on the doll is so contradictory that it is difficult to determine whether he is a representation of one of the eastern tribes or merely derived from there. The doll is rarely seen even in earlier collections.

When contemporary carvings of the doll are made, they are usually more elaborate and often have the attributes of more than one kachina combined. Undoubtedly this is because the kachina is an antique.

HANO MANA
Tewa Girl

Hano Mana appears in the Bean Dance and as a sister to many of the eastern-derived kachinas such as the Hokyang Anak' china. The effigy of this kachina maid is given to the girls in Tewa much the same as Hahai-i Wuhti is given to the Hopi girls. The doll is a favorite for the first or second gift to the infants of either group.

SIOK'CHINA
Zuñi Kachina

This kachina represents the Zuñi people and not a Zuñi kachina. He appears in the Mixed Dances in the plaza of all of the villages carrying a rattle in his right hand and a tray in his left. Dolls of this kachina are not often carved, and when they are, they are frequently confused with the Tasap or one of the Hornet Kachinas. This small doll is characteristic of those rapidly turned out that sell for a cheap price. The majority of the cutting is done with a saw, and then they are rapidly shaped with a knife. They are not lathe turned and are as accurate in their simplicity as many larger dolls. They are seldom signed.

ADDITIONAL KACHINAS

Komanshi Kachina	Kipok Kachina	Santo Domingo Kachina
Ketowa Bisena	Naastadji	Zuñi Kachina Uncle
Keresan Kachina		

Runner Kachinas or Wawash Kachinum

THE WAWASH KACHINUM are racing kachinas who appear during the spring dances to run with the men of the villages. Usually there is a group of these kachinas at one end of the plaza prancing up and down and making short dashes to get in shape. A short distance in front of them is a starting line. The man who is challenged by these kachinas is allowed to reach that mark before the race begins. However, as soon as he reaches it he is off like a shot with the kachina after him. If he escapes the kachina by the end of the village street he is given a prize, usually some form of bread. However, should the kachina win there is punishment in store for the unfortunate loser. Various reasons are cited for this particular event. Some Hopi say it is just for fun and is a race and nothing more. But there are religious overtones and other Hopi have said that "as the men race so the water will rush down the arroyos." The water is sent by the kachinas to pay the men back for their cooperation. Runner Kachinas are characterized by overly large eyes, usually round, for better vision and by abbreviated clothing, to allow better movement as they race.

KEY TO COLOR PLATE 13
   Hopi Name, *English,* (Colton #)

A. Tsil Kachina, *Chili Kachina,* (182)

B. Aya, *Rattle Runner,* (48 a)

C. Aya, or Tuskiapaya, *Rattle or Crazy Rattle Kachina,* (48b)

D. Puchkofmok' Taka, *Throwing Stick Man,* (52)

E. Hemsona, Homica, *"He Cuts Your Hair," Hair Hungry,* (51)

F. Palavitkuna, *Red Kilt Runner,* (57)

TSIL KACHINA
Chili Kachina

This runner wears chili peppers on his head, and if he catches the ones whom he races against he stuffs chili pepper in their mouths. The payment is piki bread, the same as for most runners.

AYA KACHINA a.
Rattle Runner
TUSKIAPAYA KACHINA b.
Crazy Rattle Kachina

Both of these figures are Rattle Kachinas. The white-faced one is the most common form. The runner with the black and white blocks across the head is a form called the Crazy Rattle Runner. Both of these runners carry yucca which they use on any racer who loses, to give several hard swats. If, however, the man should win, he will be given piki bread. Carved by Wallace Honwaima.

PUCHKOFMOK TAKA
Throwing Stick Man

This runner carries two throwing sticks which he throws at the person with whom he is racing. However, instead of these being actual sticks, they are made of cloth or leather stuffed with cotton to prevent injury. Should the individual win he is given piki bread. Carved by Alfred Fritz.

KEY TO COLOR PLATE 14
Hopi Name, *English,* (Colton #)

A. Kwitanonoa, *Dung Carrier,* (247)
B. Kokopell' Mana, *Assassin Fly Girl,* (66)
C. Kona, *Chipmunk,* (56)
D. Novantsi-tsiloaka, *"He Strips You,"* (50)
E. Matya, Matyso, Sivu-i-kil Taka, *Hand, Pot Carrier Man,* (114)

74

HEMSONA, HOMICA
"He Cuts your Hair," "Hair Hungry"

This runner is one much feared because of his bloody background. The story relates that in a feud between the now ruined village of Sikyatki and Walpi this kachina was used for retaliation to avenge a killing. The kachina raced the men of Sikyatki, and when it caught the son of the village chief, it cut his throat instead of merely cutting his hair knot off. This episode led directly to the destruction of Sikyatki. Possibly the reason why this kachina is handicapped by using a mask and costume which hamper his actions is to prevent his winning too often. Carved by Lowell Talashoma.

PALAVITKUNA
Red Kilt Runner

This runner is distinctive in the color of the kilt that he wears. He carries yucca whips to use on the losers in the race and rewards the winners with piki bread. There are several variations on this kachina. Carved by Wilson Kaye.

KWITANONOA
Dung Carrier

The Kwitanonoa runner is comparable to Hemsona and Kokopell' Mana in his ability to get the best possible speed from anyone challenged. If he catches his luckless victim he stuffs dry dung in his mouth or rubs his face in it. Fortunately this kachina is not common.

KOKOPELL' MANA
Assassin Fly Girl

Very few of the racers are portrayed as women but one of the most avoided is Kokopell' Mana, the erotic counterpart of Kokopelli. Should the man that "she" gets to race with her lose, she flings him to the ground and imitates copulation to the great delight of the audience. If she loses, which is not often as the better racers take this part, she pays with piki bread. The Hopi say that a man is no good to his girl friend for a year after he has been caught by this runner. Carved by Rousseau Roy.

KONA
Chipmunk

The Chipmunk carries yucca whips with which to urge onward anyone who races against him. Should they win he gives them prizes of yellow and red piki bread. Carved by Delbert Sewemaenewa.

NOVANTSI-TSILOAKA
"He Strips You"

This runner upon catching his victim will fling him to the ground and rip off the loser's clothes or failing in that may merely rip the shirt off the luckless individual. Payment will be piki bread should the man win.

MATYA, MALATSMO, MALACHPETA, MATYSO, SIVU-I-KIL TAKA
Hand Kachina, Hand Mark Kachina, Pot-Carrier Man Kachina

Matya is the runner form of the Sivu-i-kil Taka, or the Pot-Carrier, who appears in the Mixed Dances. As a runner he wears a minimum of clothing but the same symbol of a hand on his face. He carries yucca whips with which he beats the loser.

ADDITIONAL RUNNERS

Chilikomato	Kopon	Pachok'china	Sikya Taka
Chöqapölö	Letotobi	Sakwats Mana	Sivuftotovi
Kisa	Nuitiwa	Scorpion	Wik'china

Clowns or Chuchkut and Non-Kachinas

THE ROLE OF THE CLOWNS among the Hopi is a complex one for they intergrade with the serious kachinas. It is just as common to have sacred kachinas behave in a comic fashion as it is to have clowns behave ritually. The clowns' primary function is one of amusement for the audience during pauses in kachina dancing or as a leavening for the seriousness of a major ceremony. Often times there is an object lesson on improper behavior or a social commentary present in the skits and the actions of the clowns. In addition there are clowns who function as priests and others as doctors or curers. In many instances it is difficult to tell whether the impersonation should be labeled clown or kachina. Some clowns have been borrowed from neighboring tribes or inspired by them and others are unique to the Hopi.

There are dolls carved nowadays that are not kachinas; nevertheless they are often more popular than most of the kachina dolls. Foremost in this category is the Snake Dancer. Other figures such as the Mountain Spirit Dancer of the Apache, the Butterfly Girl, and the various society personages may also be carved. It is not unusual to see Lakon Manas, Two-Horned Priests, or often just a figure such as a Hopi farmer sitting in his field, or a Hopi maiden, carved in the manner of a kachina doll.

KEY TO COLOR PLATE 15

Hopi Name, *English,* (Colton #)

A. Kwikwilyaka, *Mocking Kachina,* (107)
B. Ho-e, *no English translation,* (40)
C. Tasavu, *Navajo Clown,* (—)
D. Koshari, Paiyakyamu, *Hano Clown, Glutton,* (60)
E. Koyemsi, *Mudhead,* (59)

KWIKWILYAKA
Mocking Kachina

The Mocking Kachina has no personality of his own but merely reflects the actions of anyone who passes within his view. The humor of his action lies in the rapidity with which he imitates others and their efforts to get away from him. He is usually seen in the Bean Dance as a foil for the Ho-e. The Ho-e finally rid themselves of this nuisance by pretending to set fire to their hair. The Kwikwilyaka imitates this action and touches off his cedar bark hair. Carved by Clifford Bahnimptewa.

HO-E
No English translation

Ho-e is one of the principal characters in the Bean Dance parade on First and Second Mesa. His antics are the delight of the crowds as he fights with the Mocking Kachina or runs afoul of the guards. A favorite pastime is imitating the songs and actions of others usually with little regard for the important kachinas he accompanies. He is loud and boisterous and totally lacking in any sense or responsibility. Carved by Rousseau Roy.

TASAVU
Navajo Clown

The Navajo Clown is one of long standing among the Hopi. He performs much as the Piptuka does appearing during a pause in the dance to perform some inanity. In recent years his effigy has been made more frequently and is often present in collections. Carved by Henry Talayumptewa.

KEY TO COLOR PLATE 16
Hopi Name, *English,* (Colton #)

A. Köcha Mosairu, *White Buffalo,* (—)
B. Chusona, *Snake Dancer,* (—)
C. Huhuwa, *Cross-Legged Kachina,* (125)
D. Tsuku, *Hopi Clown,* (62)
E. Piptuka, *Caricature,* (61)

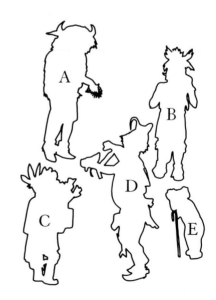

KOSHARI, PAIYAKYAMU, HANO CHUKUWAI-UPKIA
Hano Clown, Glutton

The multiple names of this clown give some indication of his origin. Koshari or variants of them may be found in most of the pueblos. They are figures that are both sacred and profane. Their actions while highly amusing are not what the Hopi or anyone else would like to be caught doing in public. They are the ultimate example of overdoing everything they set about. The doll carvers usually catch this attribute when they produce Kosharis.

KOYEMSI
Mud Head

The Koyemsi is a multi-faceted clown introduced from Zuñi. They may appear as a chorus, and on First Mesa and possibly other villages their songs are in Zuñi. During the rests in a dance they may engage in games with the boys and girls in the audience. At other times only a single Mudhead may appear as a drummer for a group. Should a dancer not have the proper mask or be late in arriving he can easily become a Mudhead by donning that mask. These kachinas appear in almost every Hopi dance. Carved by Henry Shelton.

KÖCHA MOSAIRU
White Buffalo Dancer

The White Buffalo is not a kachina but rather a social dancer who usually may be seen in the month of January on Second Mesa. The doll is a recent addition to the repertoire of carvers. It was given its popularity through the carving of Alvin James Makya who seems to have made the first examples. It is now a favorite of many carvers and collectors. Carved by Walter Hamana.

CHUSONA
Snake Dancer

The Snake Dancer is mistakenly taken for a kachina by many. It is not, being rather a society personage, but one of great popularity. The Snake Dance has always had an intense fascination for the non-Hopi and in consequence effigies of this personage have been carved for many years. Carved by Peter Shelton.

HUHUWA
Cross-Legged Kachina

This kachina is supposed to represent a Mishongnovi man who was badly crippled but of such a kind and gentle spirit that he was made a kachina. He moves about during the Powamu delivering presents to the children as he hobbles along and making wisecracks to all and sundry. He also appears during the Mixed Dances.

TSUKU
Hopi Clown

The Tsuku, like the Koshari, have a ritual pattern of behavior which they follow as they enter the village. They come in over the rooftops as though they were traversing great mountains and valleys. Making their way to the plaza they encounter incredible difficulties along the way, arriving more by accident than careful planning. Once in the plaza they build a "house" of ashes and put their "sister," a stuffed coot, inside it. Their every action is untutored and irresponsible, as they don't know how to pray to the kachinas and must learn as the kachina dance proceeds. Their actions are so unbridled that eventually kachina warriors come and threaten them for their misbehavior. Exhibiting exaggerated cowardice they blame everyone but themselves, and then when the warriors withdraw they forget it all. However, before the dance is ended the warriors return and thoroughly beat the clowns, drenching them with water as the clowns cower and promise to behave better. This play is re-enacted every time they appear, always interlarded with other humorous essays or interactions with kachinas, racers and audience. Carved by Wilfred Tewawina.

PIPTUKA
Caricature

The Piptuka are not kachinas. They have been called grotesques, clowns and comics but could just as easily be called caricatures. They are an off-the-cuff as it were, ad-lib dramatization of Hopi humor. They can be produced in a moment using the materials at hand and are then presented as humorous comments on Hopi subjects. They may appear as a skit about the rude behavior of Anglos or mimicking Hopi marital problems or whatever topic is current in the villages. There are both male and female Piptuka with the female being called Piptu Wuhti.

ADDITIONAL KACHINAS/CLOWNS

Hahai-i Wuhti	Kököle	Mastop	White Cloud Clown
Heheya	Masau'u	Owanga-zrozro	

83

Borrowed Kachinas

LARGE NUMBERS of kachinas circulate through the pueblos from east to west and back again. These are kachinas that are borrowed because of their popularity and are passed from one group to another, moving as surely as if they were alive. The Hopi have many of these kachinas, some of whose origins are well known and others that are recognized as being borrowed but from unknown origins. The majority of these kachinas are borrowed from Zuñi, the Hopi's closest pueblo neighbor. The kachinas are borrowed because they appear particularly efficacious in bringing rain or in exercising their other attributes. For some, their popularity is immediate and they are adopted, and then their appeal wanes and the kachina falls into disuse, present only in the older collections. Usually these kachinas are transferred without the folktales or depth of religious knowledge that would be possessed in their home territory. In other cases the kachina is borrowed and immediately undergoes a process of change to make the kachina look more like other Hopi kachinas.

KEY TO COLOR PLATE 17
  Hopi Name, *English,* (Colton #)

A. Poli Sio Hemis Kachina, *Zuñi Hemis Butterfly Kachina,* (246)
B. Tasap Yeibichai Kwa-um, *Navajo Talking God Grandfather,* (139)
C. Angak'china, *Long-Haired Kachina,* (127)
D. Hemis Kachina, *Jemez or Ripened Corn Kachina,* (132)
E. Saiastasana, *Zuñi Rain Priest of the North,* (154)

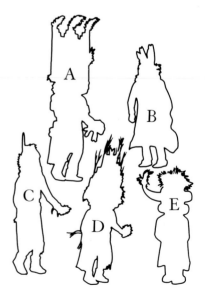

POLI SIO HEMIS KACHINA
Zuñi Ripened Corn Butterfly Kachina or Zuñi Hemis Butterfly Kachina

This kachina is reputedly from Jemez rather than Zuñi. However, many Hopi feel that it is related to a butterfly and ripened corn rather than being an actual kachina derived from the pueblo of Jemez. It appears in the ordinary Plaza Dances.

TASAP YEIBICHAI KWA-UM
Navajo Talking God Grandfather

This kachina is taken directly from the Navajo Yeibichai ceremony. The figure among the Navajo holds a position of great reverence. However, among the Hopi the kachina is given a sly twist. The personage is exaggerated both in actions and role. The entire performance is in pantomime, but the actions are just enough overdone to produce a humorous rather than serious kachina.

ANGAK'CHINA
Long-Haired Kachina

The Long-Haired Kachina is a bringer of gentle rains and flowers. He is the Kokokshi of Zuñi and yet he appears in almost all of the pueblos from the Hopi to the Rio Grande. His songs are melodic and the dance a beautiful one to see in the springtime and is a favorite of the Hopi. The dancers' long hair worn loose down the back resembles the falling rain with the eagle breast plumes rising like clouds above it. These kachinas are occasionally used for the Niman Ceremony on First Mesa. Many varieties of this kachina exist:

KEY TO COLOR PLATE 18
Hopi Name, *English*, (Colton #)

A. Üshe, *Hano Cactus*, (204)
B. Koroasta, *no English translation*, (173)
C. Sio Hemis, *Zuñi Hemis or Zuñi Ripened Corn Kachina*, (155)
D. Payik'ala, *Three-Horned Kachina*, (168)
E. Hakto, *Wood-Carrying Kachina*, (153)

Katoch Angak'china, *Barefoot Long-Haired Kachina*
Hokyan Angak'china, *Bounding Long-Haired Kachina*
Tasap Angak'china, *Navajo Long-Haired Kachina*
Tewa Angak'china, *Tewa Long-Haired Kachina, Red Bearded*
Talawipik' Angak'china, *Lightning Long-Haired Kachina*

HEMIS KACHINA
Jemez Kachina

The Hemis Kachina is most often used for the Niman or Home-Going Ceremony when the kachinas leave for six months. It is one of the most appropriate kachinas for this farewell as it is the first kachina to bring mature corn to the people, indicating that the corn crop is assured. The kachinas appear with their manas in a double line which slowly rotates in opposite directions and then back again. The Niman is one that many visitors see as their first Hopi dance, and it leaves an indelible impression of stately figures in a solemn performance of great beauty.

SAIASTASANA or SAIASTASA
Zuñi Rain Priest of the North

This kachina was borrowed from Zuñi in accompaniment with many of the other Zuñi Shalako figures. Most of these kachinas appear to have accompanied the Asa Clan when the people migrated from Zuñi and began the village of Sichomovi. This kachina is most often seen during the month of January on First Mesa when the Pamuya dances are held.

ÜSHE
Hano Cactus Kachina

Üshe appears with a Koyemsi or other clowns at Hano and reputedly belongs to the Tewa. He is a tease more than a clown or at best a practical joker. He holds a role of piki in his hand but when an unsuspecting person reaches for it he quickly substitutes cactus and holds that out for the person to prick his fingers. The Navajo have a smiliar figure called Hush-yei or Chaschin-yei and the kachina may well have derived from them rather than the Tewa. Carved by Wilbert Talashoma.

KOROASTA, KOROSTA
No English translation

Koroasta is a Keresan Kachina from the Rio Grande pueblos where his name is Akorosta. He carries a planting stick and seeds much as does his homologue Kwasai Taka on Third Mesa. He is supposed to have influence over the planting of seeds and the audience is always anxious to receive seeds from this kachina when he dances. Kwasai Taka is a related kachina that is seen more often on Third Mesa, where it is a chief kachina, than the other two mesas. Its function is the same but it differs in costume, although the face mask is quite similar.

SIO HEMIS
Zuñi Hemis

Sio Hemis is the Zuñi form of the Hemis Kachina as interpreted by the Hopi. In Zuñi it is known as the Hemishikwe Kachina. It wears the towering tableta bearing symbols of flowers and rain much as does the tableta of the Hopi Hemis Kachina. It may be used at the Niman Ceremony but usually the Hopi feel they should use their own version rather than an import. He does not appear with the other Zuñi kachinas that come in January but is more often seen in the early summer.

PAYIK'ALA, PAHIALA
Three-Horned Kachina

The Three-Horned Kachina is presumably an import from Zuñi although many Hopi claim it as an original kachina. It is most popular in the Mixed Dances on First Mesa.

HAKTO
Wood Carrying Kachina

Yamuhakto came from Zuñi sometime in the last hundred or so years. In being borrowed he lost the first part of his name and became simply Hakto Kachina. He accompanies the Sio Shalako when it is performed or appears in the Mixed Dance. Carved by Wilson Kaye.

Awatovi Soyok Taka	Hoho Mana	Matya	Sio Shalako
Awatovi Soyok Wuhti	Hututu	Naastadji	Sipikne
Chakwaina	Kahaila	Paiyakyamu	Situlili
Chaveyo	Kawaika-a	Pautiwa	Tasap
Fish Kachina	Keresan	Peacock Kachina	Teuk
Fringe Mouth God	Komanchi	Samo' Wutaka	Tiwenu
Hano Bear Clan	Koyemsi	Santo Domingo	Ursisimu
Hapota	Loi-isa	Sio Avachhoya	Wik'china
Hilili	Marao		

Bird Kachinas or Chiro Kachinum UM . . . .

BIRDS HAVE ALWAYS played a very important part in Hopi ceremonies. Their feathers decorate altars, kachinas, deities and men. Initiates into the Hopi tribe are called by the names of certain birds. Birds assist the Hopi in many endeavors. Myth has it that the strong birds of prey taught the Hopi many mysteries and helped them out of the Underworld. These birds still offer advice and council to the Hopi and remain a strong link with the mythical earlier worlds and their spirit inhabitants. Other birds are associated with water such as the snipe, the heron or crane, and ducks. These have a strong attraction for the Hopi because they stay where there is water.

For centuries birds such as the parrot or scarlet macaw have been traded out of Mexico to the Pueblo people for use in their ceremonies. Birds of all varieties occupy a position among the Hopi that is probably unsurpassed in importance by any other North American tribe.

The Bird Kachinas that appear are varied in their roles. The Owl Kachina, for example, serves as a warrior and helps to reprimand the clowns; the Crow Kachina does the same. Others are runners vying with the men and boys of the village in racing. Still others are prayers for an increase in the birds which they represent. The Duck Kachina is a prayer for the filling of the ponds wherein the ducks live and eat. Again, each kachina impersonation has the function of bringing moisture along with the other duties it performs. Several of the bird kachinas are among the older versions of kachinas, such as the Hopinyu, or the very latest, the Quail. Each is important and must fulfill its duties or obligations to the Hopi by bringing moisture, whipping clowns, and performing their individual roles.

KWAHU KACHINA
Eagle Kachina

The Eagle Kachina appears most often in the Kiva or Repeat Dances of early March. The dance is a conscious effort to duplicate the actions and motions of eagles and is a prayer for an increase of eagles. Eagles occupy a rather unique position among the Hopi, for they are treated as honored guests and are given presents just as the Hopi children are. At midsummer, however, they are ceremonially smothered and plucked of all their plumage. The kachina, with its out-stretched wings, is a favorite for doll carvers, and countless dolls are made each year. Formerly these effigies were made with real wings from small birds but nowadays the wings are entirely of wood.

KISA KACHINA
Prairie Falcon Kachina

The Prairie Falcon appears as a runner during the Soyohim dances of early spring. It is believed that the kachina is a particularly rapid runner because the Prairie Falcon flies so rapidly. Folktale has it that the Prairie Falcon brought the Hopi the first throwing stick which it modeled after the shape of its own wing. Dolls of this kachina are not very common but have had a recent surge of popularity.

PAWIK'CHINA
Duck Kachina

The Pawik Dance is a prayer for rain and pools of water. It was formerly danced more often than today. The Pawik'china may also appear in the Mixed Dance

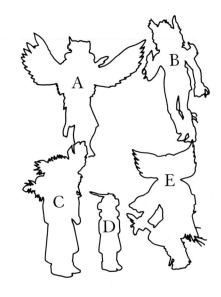

KEY TO COLOR PLATE 19
Hopi Name, *English,* (Colton #)

A. Kwahu Kachina, *Eagle Kachina,* (71)
B. Kisa Kachina, *Prairie Falcon Kachina,* (72)
C. Pawik'china, *Duck Kachina,* (75)
D. Kyash Kachina, *Parrot Kachina,* (190)
E. Mongwu, *Great Horned Owl,* (78)

as a single kachina. There are three varieties of duck kachinas, the Hopi Duck as shown, a Zuñi Duck and a form of Wukokötö seldom seen nowadays. The dolls of all of these kachinas are uncommon. The Wukokötö resembles a Tasap Kachina more than any other, but it may come in several colors. It carries a staff and resembles the Ma-alo Kachina in its actions. It is said to bring a gentle rain without thunder. The Zuñi Duck is much closer in appearance and action to the Hopi Duck although it may have a black body.

KYASH KACHINA
Parrot Kachina

The history of the Parrot Kachina is rather strange for he was apparently danced on First Mesa before the turn of the century and then never reappeared there. In 1965, a Parrot Dance was given on Second Mesa after an absence of unknown duration but the kachina did not resemble the First Mesa form. The First Mesa Kyash Kachina wore a painted parrot head on each cheek of the mask. Third Mesa has no known examples of a Parrot Kachina nor are there any in the older collections. The Kyash Kachina appeared in the Water Serpent Ceremony on First Mesa and in the Line Dance on Second Mesa.

MONGWU KACHINA
Great Horned Owl Kachina

The Great Horned Owl Kachina is a constant favorite of kachina carvers, and the ingenuity shown in making the heads of these dolls is to be marveled at. The materials range from variegated fur, rabbit skins, feathers, and wood to produce

KEY TO COLOR PLATE 20
Hopi Name, *English,* (Colton #)

A. Kowako Kachina, Takawe-e Kachina, *Chicken Kachina, Rooster Kachina,* (82)
B. Kakashka, *Quail Kachina,* (—)
C. Tocha Kachina, *Hummingbird Kachina,* (76)
D. Angwusi, *Crow Kachina,* (—)
E. Hospoa Kachina, *Road Runner Kachina,* (201)

94

an effect of owl feathers. The kachina is a warrior who disciplines the clowns when their behavior becomes too outrageous.

KOWAKO KACHINA, TAKAWE-E KACHINA
Chicken Kachina, Rooster Kachina

The Kowako Kachina is probably a recent addition to the Hopi roster of kachinas, but certainly post-Spanish. The Spanish introduced chickens into the Southwest although the Hopi did not get them until quite late. The name of this kachina should be corrected, for a Rooster Kachina is Takawe-e while a Chicken Kachina is called Kowako. A delightful folktale relates how in competition with the Mockingbird the Rooster lost his girl friend. The kachina appears during the winter Kiva Dances and Repeat Dances of March as well as appearing as a favorite in the Mixed Dances. Carved by Wallace Honwaima.

KAKASH KACHINA
Quail Kachina

The Quail Kachina is a very recent revival of an old kachina. Its reappearance occurred in the mid–1960s and was reputedly sparked by the dream of a Hopi man. There was an immediate increase in the varieties of Quail Kachinas and Quail Kachin' Manas following the first performance. However, the form of the kachina that remained after the flurry of varieties is very similar to an older doll made around 1900 that is currently in an Eastern museum.

TOCHA KACHINA
Hummingbird Kachina

The Hummingbird Kachina is a favorite impersonation during the Kiva Dances of winter or during the Soyohim Dances of springtime. The kachina bobs and calls like a bird while it moves with great rapidity. He may also appear as a runner because he moves so fast. When he catches an individual he whips him with yucca leaves. This doll is frequently made. Carved by Wallace Honwaima.

ANGWUS KACHINA
Crow Kachina

Like the Owl Kachina, Angwusi the Crow is a warrior against the clowns during the springtime dances. He threatens the clowns with retribution for their outrageous behavior and finally descends upon them with the other warriors to chastise them thoroughly. The Crow Kachina is seldom represented in the older collections, but seems to be currently increasing in number.

HOSPOA KACHINA
Road Runner Kachina

The Road Runner Kachina appears in the Kiva Dances or Mixed Dances. Road Runners are desired for their feathers which are used in making certain kinds of prayer plumes. They may formerly have also been used as guards against witchcraft. Usually dolls of this kachina are made only on order.

Additional Kachinas

Angwushahai-i	Mong' Wuhti	Tawa Koyona
Angwusnasomtaka	Palakwayo	Turposkwa
Hotsko	Potsro	Yapa
Koyona	Salap Mongwu	

Animals or Popkot

THE ANIMALS ARE the advisors, doctors and assistants of the Hopi. It is through the assistance of the animals that the Hopi have overcome monsters and cured strange diseases. In fact, the greatest doctor of them all is the Badger for it is he who knows all of the roots and herbs and how to administer them. The Bear shares in this ability. Other animals are warriors and know the ways of danger and can aid the men in becoming like them. All animals, however, share one attribute which is that they can remove their skins at will and hang them up like clothes. When they do they appear exactly as men, sitting about in their kivas, smoking and discussing serious matters. They are the Hopi's closest neighbors and are always willing to assist if approached in a proper manner and asked for help. When prayer feathers and meal are not given they often withdraw until proper behavior is forthcoming.

The Animal Kachinas thus represent the relationship present between the Hopi and the kachina spirits which some may compare to a true friendship on the human level. It involves an exchange of special favors in their interaction, accompanied by an exchange of respectful gestures.

KEY TO COLOR PLATE 21
  Hopi Name, *English,* (Colton #)

A. Kweo, *Wolf,* (86)
B. Wakas Kachina, *Cow Kachina,* (94)
C. Mosairu, *Buffalo,* (93)
D. Hon, *Bear,* (87)
E. Chöp/Sowi-ing Kachina, *Antelope/Deer Kachina,* (90b)

KWEO KACHINA
Wolf Kachina

The Wolf Kachina appears as a side dancer who accompanies the herbivorous animals such as the Deer Kachina and the Mountain Sheep Kachina in the Soyohim Dances. He often clasps a stick in his hands which represents the bushes and trees that he hides behind as he stalks his prey. At the end of one of these dances the Hopi cast meal upon him and offer prayer feathers that they might also secure game using his prowess as a hunter. Dolls of this kachina are, in contemporary times, elaborated with great teeth, lolling tongues and real fur that did not adorn the older dolls. There is almost always a Wolf Kachina on the shelf for purchase. Carved by Gilbert Naseyouma.

WAKAS KACHINA
Cow Kachina

The Cow or Wakas Kachina is a comparatively late kachina. It was reputedly conceived and introduced by a Hano man around the turn of the century. The kachina enjoyed a long run of popularity right after its introduction and then again in recent years. The name is derived from the Spanish word *vacas* for cows. The kachina is danced to bring an increase in cattle. Carved by Arthur Yowytewa.

MOSAIRU KACHINA
Buffalo Kachina

The Buffalo Kachina is not the same figure as that seen in the social dance (*see* White Buffalo, p. 82) that has been carved in recent years. It is a kachina

KEY TO COLOR PLATE 22
Hopi Name, *English,* (Colton #)

A. Chöp Kachina, *Antelope Kachina,* (90a)
B. Pong, *Mountain Sheep,* (92)
C. Kawai-i Kachina, *Horse Kachina,* (181)
D. Honan, *Badger,* (89a)
E. Honan, *Badger,* (89b)

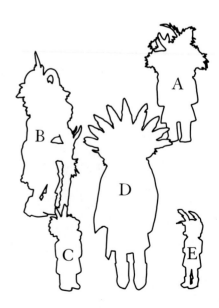

and is masked. Formerly these were made with a green face as well as one in black but in recent years the former has all but disappeared. It appears in the Plaza Dance usually with the Mixed Kachinas. Carved by Carl Sulu.

HON KACHINA
Bear Kachina

There are a number of Bear Kachinas. Some are distinguished only by color such as the Blue, White, Yellow or Black Bear Kachinas. There are others such as Ursisimu, who have become extinct, and Ketowa Bisena, who is the personage that belongs to the Bear Clan at Tewa. There are Bears fancifully dressed and Bears that are not. All Bear Kachinas are believed to be very powerful and capable of curing bad illnesses. They are also great warriors. Bear Kachinas appear most often in the Soyohim or Mixed Dances of springtime or occasionally as side dancers for the Chakwaina Kachinas. Carved by Larson Onsae.

CHÖP-SOWI-ING KACHINA
Antelope–Deer Kachina

This kachina points up the similarity of the Deer and Antelope Kachinas because by exchanging the antelope horns for deer antlers the doll would become a Deer Kachina. Both Antelope and Deer may wear shirts, usually in cold weather, and either may have a white or blue face. Formerly the attributes of each were more rigidly separated than today.

CHÖP KACHINA
Antelope Kachina

The Antelope Kachina appears in the Plaza Dances either as a group in the Line Dance or as an individual in the Mixed Dance. He, as well as all other herbivorous animals, makes the rains come and the grass grow. He usually dances with a cane held in both hands and accompanied by the Wolf Kachina as a side dancer. Carved by Gilbert Naseyouma.

PONG KACHINA
Mountain Sheep Kachina

The Mountain Sheep Kachina appears in Line Dances or as an occasional figure in the Mixed Dance. It dances holding a cane in both hands to represent the forelegs as it bends over and moves through the steps. The kachina has power over the rain as do the other herbivorous animals and is able to cure spasms as well.

KAWAI-I KACHINA
Horse Kachina

The Horse Kachina derives its name from the Spanish word for horse, *caballo*. The kachina is of recent introduction as the Hopi did not adopt the horse until quite late, preferring the burro as a beast of burden, and their own two feet if speed was desired. Early travelers through Hopi country had difficulty with Hopi guides on foot setting a pace that soon exhausted their horses. The kachina is usually seen in Mixed Dances. Carved by Kendrick Coochyumptewa.

HONAN KACHINA
Badger Kachina

The Hopi have two distinct forms of the Badger Kachina. This form is characteristic of Second Mesa and is a Chief Kachina who appears during the Powamu and the Pachavu ceremonies. It is a curing kachina. The costume and gear are not a fancier version of the other kachina but are instead of a form which probably arrived at a different time. There is some confusion on Third Mesa with the Sio Hemis Hu. However, that kachina does not have Badger tracks on its cheeks. Carved by Mac Laban.

HONAN KACHINA
Badger Kachina

This doll, characteristic of the smaller and more rapidly manufactured effigies, is also a Honan or Badger Kachina. It is more often seen during the Mixed Dances on Third Mesa or the Water Serpent Ceremony on First Mesa than during the Powamu. It bears a superficial resemblance to the Squirrel Kachina.

ADDITIONAL KACHINAS

Toho	Lakan	Poko	Mösa
Tokoch	Kona	Sikyataiyo	Ketowa Bisena

Plant Kachinas or Tusak Kachinum

PLANTS ARE of great importance to the Hopi, particularly corn which is the staple food. Wild plants formerly supplemented their diet as well. However, all plants are not given kachina form although a Hopi could use any one for a kachina impersonation. Corn Kachinas are the most common form, as might be expected. These corn impersonations may be borrowed from other Indians, convey attributes of corn or even circumstances surrounding the production and use of corn. The Hopi recognize two varieties of kachinas which are quite distinct: the Corn Dancers who wear abbreviated costumes, and the Corn Kachinas who are more elaborately dressed. Other plants are given specific form as needed or are included in the attributes of kachinas that are not basically plants.

Because rainfall and the production of plants are more immediately linked in desert areas than in non-desert terrain, it follows that Plant Kachinas literally bring their own water. If there is no moisture, there are no plants, and by extension should there be no plants, there will be no Hopi. Small wonder that the Corn Kachinas are so popular both in song and in dance.

KEY TO COLOR PLATE 23
Hopi Name, *English,* (Colton #)

A. Nayaiya Taka, *Swaying Man,* (—)
B. Sotung Taka, *Laguna Corn Kachina,* (—)
C. Navuk'china, *Prickly Pear Cactus Kachina,* (109)
D. Sio Avachhoya, *Zuñi Corn Kachina,* (166)
E. Patung, *Squash Kachina,* (225)

NAYAIYA TAKA
Swaying Man

Nayaiya Taka, the Swaying Man, is a comparatively recent import from the Rio Grande and wears the paint and costume characteristic of that area. His function is the same as that of all Corn Kachinas—increase. He appears in the Plaza Dances.

SOTUNG TAKA
Laguna Corn Kachina

This Corn Kachina appeared quite recently, apparently within the last twenty years. There are two main varieties that appear with each other. One is clothed and acts as the side dancer for the other who appears barechested. Some Hopi say that he comes from Santo Domingo and others aver he is from Laguna. He dances gracefully gesturing with the objects held in his hands. This form is sometimes called the Laguna Gambler.

NAVUK'CHINA
Prickly Pear Leaf Kachina

This is an old type of kachina who appears in the Mixed Kachina Dances. The cactus that it represents was formerly used by the Hopi for food. It can be accompanied by a "sister," Navuk'chin' Mana. He carries a pad or leaf of the cactus either on his head or on a stick when he appears.

KEY TO COLOR PLATE 24
Hopi Name, *English,* (Colton #)

A. Avachhoya, *Speckled Corn Kachina,* (122)

B. Ka-ë Kachina, *Corn Dancer,* (226)

C. Muzribi, *Bean Kachina,* (188)

D. I'she, *Mustard Greens,* (265)

E. Pachok'china, *Cocklebur Kachina,* (149)

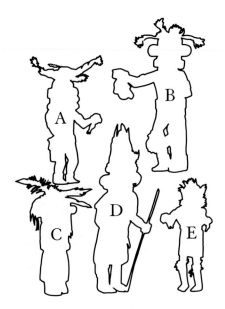

SIO AVACHHOYA
Zuñi Speckled Corn Kachina

Sio Avachhoya is a Zuñi import that appears most often on First Mesa in the Pamuya. The kachina undoubtedly came to the Hopi mesas at the same time as so many of the other Zuñi kachinas. It is often called Nawisa, which is its Zuñi name.

PATUNG KACHINA
Squash Kachina

The Squash Kachina is a Chief Kachina or *wuya* for the Pumpkin Clan. There are relatively few members of this clan left and consequently their stories are not very well known, particularly concerning their more important personages. Although the Squash Kachina's functions as a *wuya* are unknown he does appear as a runner on First Mesa according to Colton (1959, p. 69). His effigy is a great favorite for collectors, and almost all carvers produce some version of this doll.

AVACHHOYA
Speckled Corn Kachina

The Corn Kachinas called Avachhoyas come in several forms, all being distinguished by the turkey feathers on their heads which point outward in the four directions. The old style of Avachhoya was black and spotted over its body with all colors to represent the different varieties of corn. It is the younger brother of the Hemis Kachina and is usually impersonated by a young boy. Carved by Jimmie Kewanwytewa.

KA-Ë KACHINA
Corn Dancer

This kachina is one of the many Corn Dancers and is one of the most popular both for dance and song as well as function. He is a prayer for the fruition of corn and he can appear in almost every dance. The symbolism on the face is widely variable as are the colors used. His costume is more like that of the eastern pueblos. Virtually all Corn Kachinas can be distinguished by the horizontally crossed feathers on their crowns. There are numerous others that are corn dancers: Keme, from Laguna, and Yehoho, who wears a belt of roasted corn, as well as most of the Rügan Kachinas.

MUZRIBI KACHINA
Bean Kachina

The Bean Kachina is one of the Rügan or rasping kachinas that is accompanied by a mana. When he appears with a mana he is a Line Dancer, however, he is often present in Mixed Dances also. His impersonation is a prayer for an increase of beans.

I'SHE KACHINA
Mustard Greens Kachina

I'she has two distinct varieties which are so disparate that they may indeed be two distinct kachinas. Mustard greens are a wild plant collected by the Hopi for food in the spring as well as another plant called wild spinach. It is conceivable that the two kachinas represent the two plants rather than a common plant. The impersonation of the kachinas is a prayer for increase of the plant. The variety of I'she shown in Colton (1959, p. 76) resembles a warrior more than it does one of the plant kachinas. It has black warrior marks on a blue-green face and wears a standard kachina costume. The other, illustrated here, is more of a dancing variety.

PACHOK'CHINA
Cocklebur Kachina

The Pachok'china occurs in two forms. One appears in dances and the other, shown in the illustration, is a runner. The runner carries cockleburs in his hands and he puts the burrs in the hair of those he catches as the penalty for losing. The dance form of the kachina usually has a pink mask with the center portion white but the same crossed lines over the face.

ADDITIONAL KACHINAS

Hishab Kachina	Ösök'china	Tsitoto
Köcha Mana	Rügan Kachinas	Tumoala
Kokosori	Sakwap Mana	Üshe
Kopon	Samo' Wutaka	Yungya
Mashanta	Takurs Mana	Yungya Mana
Movitkun' Taka	Tsil	

Hunter Kachinas or Mahk Kachinum

THE HOPI DIVIDE almost everything in halves. Objects may be hard or soft, but so are various personages. There are summer and winter people as well as seasons. Some are warm and others cold and the same thinking applies to kachinas. Hence it is not unexpected to find the Warrior or Guard Kachinas being the hard version and the Hunter Kachinas a soft aspect. The Hunter Kachinas are conceptualized as not having the merciless nature of the Warriors. They are the hunters of game rather than men and do not usually take the position of guards or protectors of the sacred kachinas. They may appear as warriors against the clowns as does the Kipok Koyemsi.

Often the Hunter Kachinas are humorous or have unique gestures and actions that are amusing to behold. Others are fearsome in appearance, but do not necessarily live up to their mien through their behavior. Some Hunters portray members of neighboring tribes and may represent these individuals in caricature.

The Bear Kachina represents a great hunter, with the connoted attributes of power or luck implied in its impersonation. Even some of these kachinas who may seem awkward in their movements embody hunters of great skill.

KEY TO COLOR PLATE 25
   Hopi Name, *English,* (Colton #)

A. Kipok Koyemsi, *Warrior Mudhead,* (—)
B. Kahaila Kachina, *Hunter Kachina,* (145)
C. Palakwayo, *Red-Tailed Hawk,* (73)
D. Siyangephoya, *Left-Handed Kachina,* (95)
E. Hania, *Bear Kachina,* (—)

KIPOK KOYEMSI
Warrior Mudhead

The Kipok Koyemsi is a hunter of clowns and joins with the other kachinas who threaten the bumptious Chuchkut and later chastise them for their transgressions. Dolls of this kachina are not found in the earlier collections and were called Powak Koyemsi only a couple of decades ago. This is usually a sign that the kachina has not been present very long a time, for it is still regarded with suspicion. Carved by Silas Roy.

KAHAILA, KWASUS ALEKTAKA
Hunter Kachina or Man with Two Erect Feathers

Kahaila is a Mahk or Hunter Kachina rather than a Mad Kachina as he is sometimes listed. He is believed to come from the eastern pueblos. He is very close to another kachina, the Turtle. The only variance in these two is that the Turtle Kachina has a band of yellow around its head. Kahaila is made with some regularity but the Turtle Kachina is not very often seen. Carved by Arthur Yowytewa.

PALAKWAYO
Red-Tailed Hawk

Palakwayo is a Chief Kachina and appears during the Pachavu ceremony on Second and Third Mesas. He was formerly one of the group of warriors and hunters gathered by Hé-é-e during the procession at Old Oraibi. He functions both as a warrior and a hunter.

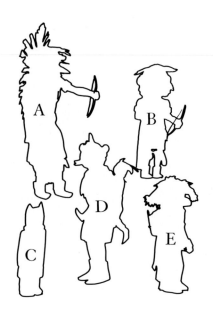

KEY TO COLOR PLATE 26
Hopi Name, *English*, (Colton #)

A. Ahote, *no English translation*, (105)
B. Tuskiapaya, *Crazy Rattle Kachina*, (258)
C. Mong' Wuhti, *Great Horned Owl Woman*, (79)
D. Tuhavi and Koyemsi, *Paralyzed Kachina and Mudhead*, (144)
E. Taha-um Soyoko, *Black Ogre's Uncle*, (30)

SIYANGEPHOYA
Left-Handed Kachina

The Left-Handed Kachina is said by some to be derived from the Hualapai Indians, but other Hopi attribute them to the Chemehuevi. He is called Left-Handed because his gear is reversed, and to draw an arrow from the quiver he must use his right hand rather than his left as is normal. The kachina moves with strange bobbings and little mincing steps. Despite his odd behavior he is supposed to be an excellent hunter. Carved by Roy Fredericks.

HANIA KACHINA
Bear Kachina

The Hania is another variety of the many Bear Kachinas. He is dressed in the manner of a warrior with two bows and arrows in one hand and a stone axe in the other. He is apparently limited to Third Mesa at the present time, and although he is referred to as ancient his doll is not present in the older collections. He is reputed to have great prowess in hunting. Carved by Rousseau Roy.

AHOTE
No English translation

This kachina's name is so close to that of another kachina, the Ho-ote, that it is often confused. Ho-ote does not resemble Ahote in any respect, for it has two black horns and a black or yellow face. Between the eyes is a multi-colored triangular patch with pendant colored circles. These circles represent the flowers of spring. The Ho-ote is a very popular kachina but it is not related to the Ahote. The Ahote Kachina appears to be derived from a Plains Indian of some variety because he wears a long trailing eagle feather headdress. The kachina appears in the Mixed Dance and is presumed to be a good hunter. Carved by Albert Bilagody.

TUSKIAPAYA KACHINA
Crazy Rattle Kachina

This kachina is undoubtedly a variant of the Sikyachantaka whose English name is either Flowers in the Snow or Guts in the Snow. Virtually the only variation between the two is the painting of the ears, for Tuskiapaya has terraced ears and Sikyachantaka does not. Legend tells that this kachina began during a time of famine among the Hopi when the Spanish had driven off all of their sheep. They were saved by a man who hunted down a cow and slaughtered it for his village. Hence the name of Guts in the Snow.

MONG' WUHTI
Great Horned Owl Woman

The kachina is not commonly performed but is reputed to appear in the night ceremonies accompanied by little owls. When she appears in these night dances during the Powamu she sings songs about hunting.

TUHAVI and KOYEMSI
Paralyzed Kachina and the Mudhead

These two kachinas enact a folktale that tells of a paralyzed man and a blind man who were left behind the other villagers during a disaster. The two combined their remaining abilities to survive. The blind man carried the paralyzed individual who served as the blind man's eyes and hunted food for them. This pair appears in the Mixed Dance. The doll is easily recognized because he is the only kachina whose horns turn down.

TAHA-UM SOYOKO
Black Ogre's Uncle

The Black Ogre's Uncle accompanies the Soyoko on their rounds through the village as they intimidate children and collect food. He is considered to be the hunter who searches out the proper game. However, he behaves in the same manner as the other Soyoko.

ADDITIONAL KACHINAS

Kipok Kachina	Salap Mongwu	Tokoch Kachina
Kweo Kachina	Söhönasomtaka	Wiharu
Mongwu	Toho Kachina	Wukokala

Insect and Reptile Kachinas or Sosoyohim Kachinum

IN IMPERSONATING KACHINAS the Hopi neglect few things in their environment. Insects and reptiles occupy as important a position in the pantheon of spirits as others that might be presumed to be more important. Each, however, has a position and some power or attribute associated with it that makes it an essential kachina. Kachinas such as the Palölökong, the Water Serpent impersonation, and the far-ranging Kokopelli are important throughout the Southwest. Their inter-relationships with other tribes far surpass those of the Eagle or Horse Kachina which in their ethnocentricity the non-Hopi might deem more important. This category of beings is, in fact, more often found represented on altars and in ceremonies than most kachinas.

Sosoyohim Kachinas, as with kachinas belonging to other categories, vary in their roles. Some of them, such as the Water Serpent who represents the deity present in all bodies of water, never appear outside of the kivas. Many may also be classified as runners.

KEY TO COLOR PLATE 27
   Hopi Name, *English*, (Colton #)

A. Palölökong, *Water Serpent or Plumed Serpent Kachina*, (233)
B. Poli Mana, *Butterfly Girl*, (—)
C. Poli Taka, *Butterfly Man*, (—)
D. Saviki, *no English translation*, (121)
E. Kuwan Kokopelli, *Colored Assassin Fly Kachina*, (—)

116

PALÖLÖKONG
Water Serpent or Plumed Serpent Kachina
This being has a ceremonial form that never appears outside of kivas and is truly snake-like. It is a representation of the water deity that occupies all bodies of water. Palölökong also has a kachina form recognizable by the small images of the deity painted on its cheeks. This figure does appear in the Mixed Dance or in the Kiva Dances. It is not often carved as a doll, for it is believed that it can cause swollen stomachs.

POLI MANA
Butterfly Girl
This effigy represents the female in the Butterfly social dance. It is not the same as the Palhik Mana although its name is often incorrectly combined with the latter to produce the name Polik Mana. In appearance it is sufficiently like the Pahlik Mana to add to the confusion. However, the face of the Poli Mana is not masked other than the bangs which cover the eyes. When the dance is given, the girls dancing are considered to appear as butterflies.

POLI TAKA
Butterfly Man
The Poli Taka is the man in the Butterfly Social Dance. Most often the doll itself is simply that of a male Butterfly Dancer, unmasked but wearing a tableta. In this instance the figure shown is an effigy from a variation of the dance that was given only one time. The addition of wings may have contributed to

KEY TO COLOR PLATE 28
  Hopi Name, *English,* (Colton #)

A. Tatangaya, *Hornet Kachina,* (68)
B. Kokopelli, *Assassin Fly Kachina,* (65)
C. Puchkofmok' Taka, *Scorpion Kachina,* (52)
D. Susöpa, *Cricket Kachina,* (64)
E. Lölökong, *Racer Snake Kachina,* (—)

its lack of popularity. As is common with the carvings of the Poli Taka, this doll is also masked, unlike the dancers themselves.

SAVIKI, CHANU KACHINA
No English translation

Saviki is a Chief Kachina on First Mesa where he appears in the Powamu procession. He is one of the *wuya* of the Snake Clan. Saviki is an extremely rare doll and is difficult to get even when ordered carved. Although his appearance does not indicate it, he is a Snake Kachina.

KUWAN KOKOPELLI
Colored Assassin Fly Kachina

Many kachinas have a variety of forms in which they can appear. They may come arrayed differently when they are Morning Kachinas from their afternoon appearance. Others vary their ceremonial dress from their dance appearance. Still others may have a sun form or a colored form or even a *kwivi* (sporty) form. This particular doll is Kokopelli in his colored or *kuwan* form. Unfortunately the small ears are missing at either side of the head.

TATANGAYA KACHINA
Hornet Kachina

Two varieties of the Hornet Kachina exist that bear no resemblance to each other. The illustrated variety supposedly exists only on First Mesa. The other type which resembles a Tasap Kachina with colored rings about the face is presumably limited to Second or Third Mesa. It would be expectable, however, to find both forms in a Mixed Dance on all three mesas. It may be that the multi-colored form is either a recent addition or merely the Kuwan form of the Hornet.

KOKOPELLI
Assassin Fly Kachina or Humpbacked Flute Player

This kachina appears individually in the Mixed Dance and in groups in the Kiva Dances. He is equated with the Humpbacked Flute Player when he borrows a flute from Lenang, the Flute Kachina, and plays it. Despite the fact that this is the only time that he plays the flute there are other interesting similarities. Both are humped and ithyphallic. Legend relates that the Humpbacked Flute Player bears gifts in a sack on his back, seduces girls and makes his presence known by playing the flute. Another tale relates that he is the humpbacked Robber or Assassin Fly that never stops copulating. Possibly this latter tale is a reflection of an attribute of the Humpbacked Flute Player.

PUCHKOFMOK' TAKA
Scorpion Kachina

This kachina is called either the Throwing Stick Man (*see* Runners, p. 74) or the Scorpion Kachina. The scorpion's habit of flipping his tail to sting undoubtedly gave it the name of Throwing Stick Man. The kachina is primarily a runner. There is another kachina by the same name who is neither a scorpion nor a runner and appears in the Mixed Dance.

SUSÖPA KACHINA
Cricket Kachina

Susöpa has been listed in Colton (1959, p. 35) as a runner. However, all of the Hopi who have contributed information feel that it is a kiva dancer and is not supposed to appear anywhere else, although this may be a mesa difference. He is one of the few kachinas that carries nothing in his hands when he dances.

LÖLÖKONG KACHINA
Racer Snake Kachina

This kachina represents the slender desert snake called the racer. Its movements are rapid when it appears as a guard in the Powamu procession. Lölökong stands stamping in one place and then in a flash is some distance away to begin stamping again.

ADDITIONAL KACHINAS

| Mahu | Momo | Pakiowik'china | Sivuftotovi |
| Mastop | Monongya | Situlili | |

Miscellaneous Kachinas

TO A DEGREE all of the Sosoyohim Kachinas are a miscellaneous or Mixed Group. They represent the stock of kachinas that may be called upon depending on need, desire or choice. As has been previously mentioned, each has a characteristic or an attribute which he brings to aid the Hopi. Many, however, are kachinas which are undergoing a rapid change or are newly introduced. The division is not to be construed as a Hopi category and is used merely to illustrate a few eccentricities.

Some of these kachinas are heroes in folktales or have stories which they themselves may relate to villagers assembled where they appear in the kiva. Others have histories reaching back into antiquity and positions that demand their presence at a particular dance. Some are innovations that have not yet become sufficiently embedded in the Hopi kachina cycle to make them known in all villages. Many kachinas assigned to this category are spoken of simply as Sosoyohim because there is no necessity to assign them to a specific kachina grouping. The popularity and frequency of appearance of the Sosoyohim, as with other kachinas, may grow or diminish with time, and some which are presently restricted to one or two villages may eventually make appearances on all three mesas.

KEY TO COLOR PLATE 29
  Hopi Name, *English*, (Colton #)

A. Talavai Kachina, *Morning Singer Kachina*, (108)

B. Kana-a Kachina, *Sunset Crater Kachina*, (142)

C. Kuwan Heheya, *Colored Heheya*, (34)

D. Kököle, *no English translation*, (5)

E. Tawa Kachina, *Sun Kachina*, (146)

TALAVAI KACHINA
Early Morning Singer Kachina

The Talavai Kachina is also called the Silent Kachina, although it sings. It comes in pairs during the Bean Dance and stands to one side of the procession holding its small spruce tree and bell. It wears the red and white maiden's robe which is a characteristic garb for many kachinas that appear in the early morning. Carved by Clifford Bahnimptewa.

KANA-A KACHINA
Sunset Crater Kachina

The Sunset Crater Kachina is among the few kachinas that has a folktale about it. However, the tale tells of the formation of Sunset Crater but does not indicate any relationship between the kachinas and that event. Nevertheless the Hopi link the two together. The legend tells of how the people of the village of Pivanhonkyapi just north of Oraibi became wicked and would not listen to the chief. In desperation he called in the powerful medicine men, the Yaya. These individuals placed something in his corn bin and told him not to disturb it. Four days later smoke appeared on the slopes of the San Francisco Peaks. Four days after this the village was destroyed by a fire cloud that came from the northeast slope of the peaks. The location is now the home of the Kana-a Kachina. Carved by Arthur Yowytewa.

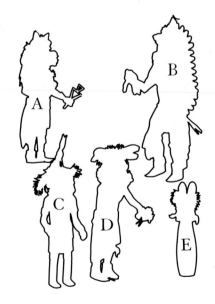

KEY TO COLOR PLATE 30
Hopi Name, *English*, (Colton #)

A. Mösa, *Cat or Old Style Navajo Kachina*, (—)

B. Nangasohu Kachina, *Chasing Star or Meteor Kachina*, (148)

C. Marao Kachina, *no English translation*, (170)

D. Na-ui-kui Taka, *Peeping Out Man (Corn)*, (235)

E. Ahulani/Kä-e Kachina, *Ahulani/Corn Kachina*, (164)

KUWAN HEHEYA
Colored Heheya

The Kuwan Heheya is a Line Dancer who occasionally appears as the Niman Kachina in place of the Hemis Kachina. He is accompanied by an uncle, the Heheya Taha-um. On Second Mesa this uncle is absent. The Sikya Heheya (*see* Ogres, p. 48) seems to be the only other form used. Undoubtedly the Kuwan Heheya does appear on all three mesas. Carved by Mark Laban.

KÖKÖLE
No English translation

This Chief Kachina varies in function between each mesa. It has been stated in the literature that it is absent on First Mesa but dolls exist to show its presence and some mention of it is made in early writings. The only similarity between mesas is in the symbolism on the face. Third Mesa Kökökölom are usually black and come in groups dressed in worn-out garb. Second Mesa Kökökölom come as a pair with yellow faces and are dressed in buckskins, while First Mesa apparently had but a single white-face Kököle dressed in a fringed hunting shirt.

TAWA KACHINA
Sun Kachina

The deity Tawa has a vast number of stories relating to its interaction with all people as well as animals and monsters. Yet the kachina form of the deity appears in the Mixed Dance as simply another of the average kachinas. It does not appear in any major ceremonial events.

MÖSA KACHINA
Cat Kachina or Old Style Navajo Kachina

This form of a Tasap Kachina is called Mösa or Cat Kachina. It is also referred to occasionally as a Black Cat Kachina. Its history is interesting because it was originally inspired by the Navajo who ran from place to place giving notification of an approaching ceremony and inviting their neighbors. The Hopi, who customarily received visits from this individual, produced a kachina called Old Navajo Kachina. This figure was borrowed from the Hopi by the Zuñi. Later it was borrowed back by the Hopi and renamed the Cat Kachina.

NANGASOHU KACHINA
Chasing Star or Meteor Kachina

According to some Hopi this kachina represents a planet but to many others it is a meteor that is the Chasing Star. The kachina wears an enormous headdress of trailing eagle feathers, carries a yucca whip and a bell and appears in pairs. Despite this unusual gear and eye-catching costume contemporary Hopi are vague as to its purpose when it appears in the Mixed Dance.

MARAO KACHINA
No English translation

The Marao Kachina was introduced in 1920 and is a figure of contradictions. It is said that the kachina came from the Zuñi but all of its costume and painting indicate that it is Navajo inspired. It wears on its head the tripod headgear belonging to the Mamzrau, a woman's society, which may account for its name. However, beneath the woman's headdress, on the cheeks of the mask are symbols of war. Dolls of this kachina are made very often.

NA-UI-KUI TAKA
Peeping Out Man (A Corn Kachina)

Peeping Out Man appeared in the early 1940s on Third Mesa presumably coming from the Santo Domingo Harvest Dancers. His name refers to the band across the lower part of the mask giving the impression of the eyes peering over this strip. The kachina is one of the many Corn Kachinas and appears in the Plaza and Kiva Dances.

AHULANI/KÄ-E
First Mesa Solstice Kachina and Corn

This form of kachina doll is relatively recent in appearance, possibly within the last three decades. It utilizes the head of virtually any kachina and superimposes it on a body that represents an ear of corn. This cylindrical shape is an easy way to avoid the lengthy task of carving the body, but it seems more likely that it is a conscious linking of kachinas and corn.

Additional Kachinas

Akush Kachina
Alosaka
Chimon Mana
Chiwap Kachina
Cross-Crowned Kachina
Dog Kachina
Field Kachina
Flute Kachina
Four Horned Kachina
Hapota
Hewani Kachin
Holi Kachina
Hochani
Kalavi

Köchaf
Kwavonakwa
Lemowa Kachina
Loi-isa
Macibol
Mahu
Makto
Maswik
Nakiachop
Nukush
Ongchomo
Ota
Pakwabi

Palongahoya
Paski Kachina
Pautiwa
Poko
Pöökong Kwivi
River Kachina
Sohu Kachina
Somaikoli
Tanakwewa
Tuma-oi Kachina
We-u-u
Yehoho
Yowe

Hopi Word Pronunciation Guide

A FEW SIMPLE RULES of pronunciation can be presented, without attempting a linguistic discussion on the intricacies of Hopi language, to aid the collector.

Vowels: The Hopi have a short and a prolonged form of every vowel, such as *ba* and *baa,* with an accompanying meaning change. In addition there is a vowel not found in English which in its short form is written *ü* and pronounced like the German *mütter* and in its long form like the French word *fleuve* and is given as *ö.*

Consonants: These are also difficult as they are often pronounced at midpoint between two of our consonants such as *b* and *p, d* and *t, s* and *sh,* or *ch* and *ts.* The orthography of these has led to a wide variation of spellings. Additionally the consonants of *k* and *n* have three modes of pronunciation, being formed at the front, middle and back of the mouth with consequent shifts of meaning. The Hopi recognizes a nasalized *n* like the Spanish *ñ* that is written in this publication as *ng,* si*ng.* Similarly *k* has a form coupled with a *y* sound to produce *ky, kya* or *kia.*

Accent: The majority of Hopi words are accented on the second syllable unless otherwise marked with the symbol *'.*

Glottal Stop: Many Hopi words are divided or broken by a glottal stop, a momentary closure of the throat such as occurs in the latter of these two phrases, "a nice man" and "an' ice man."

Elisions: Words may also be combined in Hopi, dropping a vowel in the process; thus Kachina Mana becomes Kachin' Mana and Anga Kachina becomes Angak'china.

It is too difficult to use the Hopi terms for dual, plural and paucal (a few), so all are referred to in the singular. A short discussion of Hopi linguistics may be found in the glossary of *Hopi Journal,* vol. II, 1936 by Alexander M. Stephen or in the archives at the Museum of Northern Arizona or in Whorf's writings.

The index is devised so that all Hopi kachinas are listed under their native names to avoid the inevitable confusion arising from English descriptive names, misnomers or pseudonyms.

Index

132

{ K }

{ L }

137